Art Quilt Workbook

EXERCISES & TECHNIQUES TO IGNITE YOUR CREATIVITY

JANE DÁVILA & ELIN WATERSTON

C&T PUBLISHING

Text © 2007 Jane Dávila and Elin Waterston

Artwork © 2007 C&T Publishing, Inc.

Publisher: Amy Marson

Editorial Director: Gailen Runge

Acquisitions Editor: Jan Grigsby

Editor: Deb Rowden

Technical Editors: Elin Thomas, Nanette S. Zeller

Copyeditor/Proofreader: Wordfirm

Design Director/Cover & Book Designer: Christina D. Jarumay

Illustrator: Tim Manibusan

Production Coordinators: Kirstie L. Pettersen, Zinnia Heinzmann

Photography: Luke Mulks and Diane Pedersen unless otherwise noted

Published by C&T Publishing, Inc., P.O. Box 1456, Lafayette, CA 94549

Front cover: *Leaf Study* by Jane Dávila, *Return 4* by Elin Waterston, *Tiger Fish* by Elin Waterston, and *Brilliant Anyway* by Elin Waterston

Back cover: *Playa de Paracas*, by Jane Dávila (top); bottom (from left)—*Mind & Memory (Ansonia)* by Elin Waterston; *Finial III* by Jane Dávila; *Pears: Pome(ae)*, by Elin Waterston.

Library of Congress Cataloging-in-Publication Data

Dávila, Jane.

 Art quilt workbook : exercises & techniques to ignite your creativity / Jane Dávila and Elin Waterston.

    p. cm.

  Includes index.

  ISBN-13: 978-1-57120-377-9 (paper trade : alk. paper)

  ISBN-10: 1-57120-377-X (paper trade : alk. paper)

1. Quilts--Design. 2. Art quilts. I. Waterston, Elin, II. Title.

  TT835.D372 2007

  746.46'041--dc22

2006019419

Printed in China

10 9 8 7 6

DEDICATION

for Gram…Jane
for my mother…Elin

ACKNOWLEDGMENTS

Jane & Elin would like to thank…

Jan Grigsby, Deb Rowden, Elin Thomas, Sara MacFarland, Amy Marson, Zinnia Heinzmann, Kirstie Pettersen, Diane Pedersen, Nanette Zeller, Tim Manibusan, Christina Jarumay, Luke Mulks; Paul Boylan and Lori Joseph; Claire Oehler and the staff of the Country Quilter; Linda Oehler Marx; and the student artists who made this book possible.

Jane would like to thank…

her family—especially Carlos and Samantha for their love and encouragement—Jon Stewart, and Jonathan Safran Foer.

Elin would like to thank…

her family—especially David and Alex for their patience, advice, and support—Karen Drayne, Loren Chase and the staff of the Katonah Art Center & Anderson Chase Gallery, Rhett Miller and The Old 97's, OK Go, and Todd Deatherage.

Mind & Memory (W 79th/N Main), by Elin Waterston

Contents

INTRODUCTION . . . **4**

HOW TO USE THIS BOOK . . . **5**

CHAPTER ONE: The Basics

The elements of design and composition; inspiration and creativity; working with a theme and in a series **8**

EXERCISES: *Word play; patterns and balance; contour line drawing* . . . **16**

CHAPTER TWO: Color Use, Perspective, and Border Options

The use and moods of color; simple perspective; borders and alternatives . . . **18**

EXERCISES: *Word play; warm and cool combinations; simple perspective* . . . **23**

CHAPTER THREE:
Inspiration from Images

Using photography in quilt design, computer manipulation, images as inspiration; drawing from a photograph . . . **25**

EXERCISES: *Working from a pattern—pear quilt; working from an original drawing* . . . **31**

CHAPTER FOUR: Fabric Collage

The basics of fabric collage, appliqué design and techniques . . . **36**

EXERCISES: *Color collage; collage with a focus* . . . **39**

CHAPTER FIVE: Innovative Piecing

Unusual piecing techniques . . . **41**

EXERCISES: *Freehand curves; wonky piecing; insert strips* . . . **43**

CHAPTER SIX: Paint Effects

Painting and stamping techniques, using foil . . . **48**

EXERCISES: *Abstract painting; representational painting; stamping; foiling with glue; foiling with fusible web* . . . **51**

CHAPTER SEVEN: Thread Work

Various ways of using thread as a design element . . . **56**

EXERCISES: *Thread painting; bobbin drawing; couching* . . . **60**

CHAPTER EIGHT: Found Objects

The use of found objects; archival considerations . . . **64**

EXERCISES: *Working with paper; methods of attachment* . . . **68**

CHAPTER NINE: Embellishing

An array of embellishments and their use in compositions . . . **70**

EXERCISES: *Combining embellishments; edge embellishments* . . . **76**

CHAPTER TEN: Finishing Techniques

Finishing and binding techniques and hanging methods . . . **77**

CHAPTER ELEVEN: The Business of Being an Artist

Information on exhibiting your work, marketing, and networking . . . **82**

STUDENT GALLERY . . . **87**

GLOSSARY . . . **92**

CRITIQUING EXERCISES/RESOURCES . . . **93**

INDEX . . . **94**

ABOUT THE AUTHORS . . . **95**

INTRODUCTION

Within the last decade, the quilt industry has matured as people have mastered traditional skills and designs. Some quilters have begun to look beyond traditional patterns and techniques. Although there is nothing wrong with and much to be said for making quilts to cover beds, there comes a time to step outside the box and explore the convergence of quilting and art.

While technical workmanship and skills are important in art quilting, a good grasp of design is equally important,

as is a willingness to experiment with composition and materials. Art quilting is both art and quilting—both aspects should be balanced, and yet the definitions of each should be stretched.

We hope that this book will give you a foundation in the basics of good design, show you some techniques to use in your work, help you to develop a personal style, and show you what comes next in the process of becoming an art quilter. Take what you learn and make it your own.

Sedna, by Elin Waterston

HOW TO USE THIS BOOK

Goals

This book is as much about thinking and seeing as it is about fabric and sewing. We hope that you will use this book to begin a journey toward developing your own unique artistic style and finding your "voice" as an artist.

Start the process with us by creating a series of finished art quilts. You will learn specific techniques and design skills to use in the creation of these pieces. Although you may not incorporate every new skill into your personal toolbox, we do want you to try everything. Different people will love different aspects of each chapter's lesson, but exposure to a variety of techniques will give you a range of tools to choose from when you create art quilts now—and five years from now.

The techniques presented here represent a small fraction of what is available, but they will be enough to get you started and open you to the possibilities that lie ahead. You should feel free to experiment, make mistakes, challenge yourself, and explore the potential of art quilts.

We will also provide you with the information necessary to exhibit your work. Whether exhibiting is an immediate goal or something that you haven't yet considered, please remember that information is never wasted. In the future, you may find yourself ready to take the next step in your journey.

Millie, by Elin Waterston

Basic Skills

This book addresses the *art* in art quilting and assumes a certain level of knowledge of and ability in basic quilting skills. Familiarity and competence in the following areas are expected:

- Basic cutting, sewing, and piecing
- Basic terminology
- Fusing
- Machine quilting
- Free-motion quilting

Supplies

Although it's not necessary to have the latest, most expensive gadgets and supplies, it is important to find what works for you and helps you express yourself through your art. That said, the better your equipment is, the less frustrating the working process will be. A good sewing machine, well maintained and in good working order, is invaluable. High-quality fabrics, threads, and other materials are a joy to work with and will contribute to the longevity of your work. Sturdy, thin batting (like Warm & Natural) is a good choice for art quilts because it will give them body and will hang well.

BASIC SUPPLIES

Many of these supplies will be needed for most of the exercises in this book. Some, while not absolutely necessary, can make a task easier or eliminate steps and streamline a process. Specific supplies will be addressed in each chapter.

- Rotary cutter
- Rulers in various sizes for cutting
- Cutting mat

- Scissors (for both fabric and paper)
- Sewing machine in good working order, with various feet (¼˝ piecing, open-toe embroidery, free-motion/darning, walking)
- Sewing machine needles (75/11 universal, embroidery, and quilting)
- Pins
- Nonstick appliqué pressing sheet
- Pinking shears
- Sketchbook or journal
- Drawing pencils (color and graphite)
- Eraser
- Sharpie or Identipen marker, or Pigma marking pen
- Basic sewing kit
- Drawing rulers
- Freezer paper
- Tracing paper
- Fusible web
- Stabilizer
- Various threads, both regular sewing weight and decorative
- Iron and ironing board

NICE-TO-HAVE SUPPLIES

These supplies, although not required for either art quilting or the use of this book, will allow you to explore more options and can expand your artistic horizons.

- Digital camera
- Computer with Internet access
- Scanner
- Color inkjet printer
- Design wall
- Lightbox

La Libélula, by Jane Dávila

Process of Working

We strongly recommend that you follow this book chapter by chapter in consecutive order because it is designed as a course of study, with skill building on skill in a logical order. We also suggest that you complete at least one quilt based on each of the lessons in Chapters 2–9. At the end of each chapter, we give you homework that will encourage you to work on a small series of quilts. All the quilts are to be 9˝ × 12˝ in a vertical (or portrait) orientation. We chose this size and orientation requirement for several reasons:

- The quilts are small enough that they won't be terribly time consuming.
- The small quantity of materials involved will keep you from becoming too attached to the work (it is important to learn that it is okay to abandon a piece that isn't working).

- This size gives you freedom to experiment—again because of the quantity of materials and time.

- The size requirement will give you the experience of working with arbitrary rules imposed on you from without (a necessary, recurring, real-world art experience).

Many of the exercises call for a 9″ × 12″ background as a starting point. This requirement will get you familiar with the size in terms of design composition. However, the reality of art quilting is that there is quilting, which means that when making the pieces for your homework assignments, you need to work slightly larger to allow for shrinkage during quilting or for edge-finishing techniques that can affect the finished size of the piece. Using a mask with a 9″ × 12″ opening can aid you in planning your composition and in visualizing potential framing options when it comes time to trim the piece to size.

La Avispa, by Jane Dávila

References for Further Exploration

At the end of each chapter, we list artists whose work highlights aspects of the chapter's lesson. The work of many of these artists may be relevant for more than one lesson. For example, we use Henri Matisse's later work to illustrate collage in Chapter 4 in terms of shapes, space, and color, but his work may also be useful for Chapter 2 (color) and Chapter 6 (paint). You will learn by studying the artists listed while looking for the connection to the particular lesson. The lists of artists are a starting point and are by no means meant to be complete. Look for the connection between Art (with a capital A) and art quilting.

URLS

Website addresses (URLs) are offered because they illustrate aspects of a chapter's lesson. URLs are often transitory, so some of the listed URLs may no longer be valid. If you find an invalid URL, do an Internet search using the artist's name, or keywords from the chapter, such as quilt+art+series or quilt+art+collage to find your own examples.

Some Thoughts on Copyright

- When in doubt about whether an image is copyrighted, ask permission.

- Never assume that an image is not copyrighted; always assume that it is.

- The fact that an image is old, or the creator is deceased, doesn't mean that the copyright has expired. If the heirs or the rightful owners of the copyright have renewed it, the image is protected.

- It's a myth that changing an image by at least 10 percent is a copyright loophole. Copyright law protects against derivative work as well.

- The website of the United States Copyright Office is an excellent source for definitive information regarding copyright law, http://www.copyright.gov/.

One of our main objectives is to encourage you to create your own art. Using someone else's art won't be necessary.

CHAPTER **ONE:**
THE BASICS

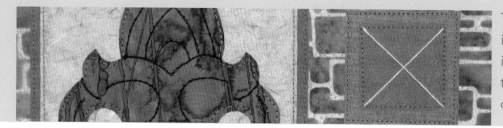

This chapter's lesson covers inspiration and creativity, working in a series and with a theme, and the elements and principles of design and composition.

"All real works of art look as though they were done in joy." —ROBERT HENRI

art, *n.* The conscious use of skill and creative imagination especially in the production of aesthetic objects (from Latin *articulus*: article).

quilt, *n.* A coverlet made of two layers of fabric with a layer of cotton, wool, feathers, or down in between held in place with tied or stitched designs (from Latin *culcita*: mattress).

Anticipation, **by Jane Dávila**

Inspiration

Inspiration is everywhere!

What inspires an artist is very personal. You must find your personal inspiration and learn how to tap into it. The most useful skill you can develop as an artist is observation. Slow down and really look at the world around you. Look again—see the relationships between objects, colors, and shapes. Learning to *see* is really important.

> **SOURCES OF INSPIRATION:**
>
> **Visual**—nature, environment and surroundings, fine art, folk art, movies, photography
>
> **Written**—literature, folktales, mythology, poetry
>
> **Auditory**—nature (again), music

Once you get inspired, you need to capture that inspiration. Some artists find it useful to carry a journal with them or keep one at their bedside to record ideas as they occur. Don't assume you'll be able to remember that brilliant idea later. You're trying to capture the gist of the idea, so a full-blown drawing is not necessary; just do a quick thumbnail sketch or write a brief description. The sketch or description will serve as a reminder of the idea to take you back to the spot where you got inspired. Even if you don't keep a formal journal, recording your ideas when they hit you is still important. This can take the form of sketching, doodling, or somehow recording first impressions on any available writing surface—paper napkins, envelopes, margins of the newspaper. View these notes as a starting point and be prepared to follow the ideas where they lead you.

Allow yourself to be open to inspiration!

Sketch, draw, doodle

The Creative Process

Every artist develops a personal work style. In this section, we describe the working styles that we use and provide some suggestions for coping with a "creative stall." You might find that one style works better for you than another, or you might find that you prefer a combination of these styles, or even some other way of working entirely. You might also find that your working style changes over time. Creativity is not a static thing—you're changing all the time, so the way you work is likely to change as well.

LET IT IN
Visual Feast

Surround yourself with a plethora of imagery. Use a bulletin board to tack up doodles, sketches, pictures torn from magazines, examples of cool fonts, paint chips, and swatches of fabric, and then add and subtract on a whim.

A bulletin board full of imagery

Visual Stimulation

Collect objects of various colors and textures—things gathered on a morning walk, items of beauty in your house, fruits and vegetables. Create an ever-changing display of visual stories.

Word Association

Play a word association game with yourself—think of a word, think of synonyms, think of the definition of the word, see where it takes you. This chain of words can lead you in unpredictable directions.

BLOCK IT OUT

Loud Music

Block out the distraction of the outside world by playing music. This auditory diversion can be helpful in stimulating other centers of your creative brain.

Crossword Puzzles

Occupy your left brain by doing something cerebral like a crossword puzzle, an acrostic, or a logic game—an intellectual task will free up your right brain for creative thoughts. Artistic ideas will flow more readily when you are not trying too hard.

Physical Activity

Another distraction technique that lets the creative side of your brain relax enough to process inspiration more clearly is physical activity.

FIND THE ZONE

Start with more than you think you'll need, and edit or add as needed.

Gathering and Editing

Collect any and all materials you think might work in your piece, without discrimination—start with way too much and whittle it down.

Trial and Error and Planned Spontaneity

Keep arranging and rearranging the fabrics, shapes, elements, and found objects in your piece. Take digital photos or sketch as you go—you'll never remember the first of 40 compositions without a reminder. Stop only when you love your design.

Respecting the Zone

Once your creative juices start to flow, you'll find you get into a "zone." It's important to respect the zone and stay in it—you might not be able to get it back. Your family will understand, and the occasional bowl of cereal for dinner will add a little spontaneity to their lives as well.

Flexibility

Be open to change. Although you might start with a careful plan, you need not stick to it. Your finished project might be dramatically different than what you envisioned —go with your gut reaction and allow the work to evolve. Accept the unforeseen as part of the process.

Arrange and rearrange things with interesting shapes, colors, and textures for inspiration.

CREATIVITY STALLS

Creativity stalls happen to everyone! In your life as an artist, you will go through more than one fallow period, when you hit a wall and have no ideas. Every artist develops coping techniques. Different techniques will work for different people at different times.

Break Your Routine

Shake up your way of working. Try a different approach— get uncomfortable. Work outside your usual color palette or subject matter. Work in a different room in your house. If you usually work in the morning, try working late at night. If you work in silence, put on some music. Think about how you work and try to vary aspects of your process.

Variations of Previous Work

Go back to the last place where you were able to be creative before the block and see whether you can head in a different direction. Once you've created a variation of a previous work, push farther from your starting point.

Mindless Exercise—Physical or Mental

You can try to get outside the stall with physical or mental exercise. Try puzzles, brain teasers, foreign language tapes—anything not related to your work or your working space.

Something Totally Different

Try something relatively mindless but still within your medium (a simple pieced baby quilt or placemats, for example), or try something completely different, yet still creative. Sign up for a ceramics class, a photography class, or even a tap dancing class! Learning a new skill can reawaken creativity in all areas.

Learning from Unsuccessful Pieces

Unsuccessful attempts are learning experiences. Every single thing you create, successful or unsuccessful, offers an opportunity to grow. Give yourself permission to discard, throw out, chop up, or otherwise destroy or transform unsuccessful pieces so they will no longer stare at you reproachfully from the corner of your studio!

Go Digital

Take digital pictures of an unsuccessful piece and manipulate those images on your computer. Converting them to grayscale or black and white, for example, will allow you to see composition and form without being distracted by color. Flip the image upside down or use the mirror image function, again forcing you to focus on composition. Distort the length, the width, or both. Crop a section and see whether a portion of the initial composition is more pleasing than the whole. Print out a picture of the piece, chop it up, and rearrange the parts.

Fish Pond, **by Elin Waterston**

Regardless of where you find inspiration, or how you translate this inspiration into fabric art, the most important thing is to do the work. Find your personal style, your voice, and create!

"Realize the value of putting down your first impression quickly." —CHARLES HAWTHORNE

Working With a Theme

Leaf Study, **by Jane Dávila**

Art created with a theme represents a specific subject or topic. A theme can be the starting point for a set of variations that is the beginning of a series. Examples of art created with a theme include a pictorial landscape quilt of the Grand Canyon or an abstract quilt of the colors of a forest fire.

Working in a Series

Finial I, by Jane Dávila

Finial II, by Jane Dávila

Finial III, by Jane Dávila

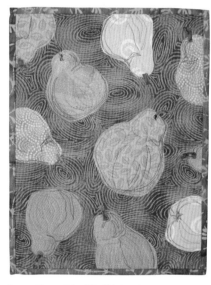

Pears: Tossed, by Elin Waterston

Pears: Pome(ae), by Elin Waterston

Pears: On a Plate, by Elin Waterston

Art created in a series can explore similarities in theme, technique, inspiration, or size, or any combination thereof. There is a commonality—a thread—that is carried through all the works that make up a series.

Working in a series allows you to pick a theme and explore it until its potential is exhausted, until everything has been said. This might happen after just two pieces—or a series can continue for a lifetime. You can work on more than one series at a time, and a series might evolve as you develop a theme.

A series can be a group of quilts based on the forms of African sculpture, or depicting Greek myths, or as homage to a particular artist, city, or event.

Visual Elements of Design

There are seven visual elements with which we create art. These elements apply to all visual art—sculpture, painting, architecture, quilting, even flower arranging. A composition is an arrangement of these elements.

COLOR

Color is a property of light—as light changes, color changes. Color has tremendous expressive potential. It can convey mood and emotion.

LINE

Line is a form of length created by movement. It can be a mark that describes a shape or outline. A curved line is more naturalistic than a straight line, which is more static. In quilting, line is most often the quilting itself, or a surface element.

LINE DIRECTION

A line's potential is to suggest movement. Line communicates through its direction. Horizontal lines are calm and passive. Vertical lines are stable and evoke strength. Diagonal lines suggest depth and movement and are more dynamic than vertical or horizontal lines.

SHAPE

Shapes can be divided into two types: organic (irregular, naturalistic) and geometric (triangles, circles, squares, and so on).

SIZE

The relative sizes of objects can be used to emphasize importance or depth. Contrast in size is useful for creating a focal point and emphasis.

VALUE

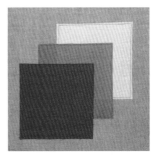

Value refers to an area's relative lightness or darkness. Value differences (low and high contrast) can create mood.

TEXTURE

Texture is the surface quality of objects. Contrast in texture provides visual interest. Texture refers to differing prints as well as to rough and smooth, shiny and matte, and so on. Texture can be visual or physical.

Visual Principles of Design

The visual principles of design are guidelines you can use to work with and arrange the elements of a composition. The organization of the elements can convey feelings and ideas and can define the intent of the work.

BALANCE

Balance refers to the distribution of the weight or emphasis of visual elements. Balance can be symmetrical, nearly symmetrical (approximate), asymmetrical (informal), or radial. Imbalance disturbs the viewer, so use a purposeful imbalance to evoke an uneasy response and engage the viewer. Placing visual weight toward the top of a composition makes it more unstable and dynamic.

Symmetrical Balance

If you draw an imaginary vertical line down the center of a composition with symmetrical balance, the two sides are equal and each is a mirror image of the other. Symmetrical balance is common in architecture. A butterfly is an example of something that exhibits symmetrical balance.

Nearly Symmetrical (Approximate) Balance

In a composition with nearly symmetrical, or approximate, balance, minor differences in color, shape, and form create a nearly mirror image on either side of an imaginary vertical line.

Asymmetrical (Informal) Balance

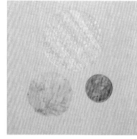

In a composition with asymmetrical, or informal, balance, dissimilar objects with equal visual weight are distributed on either side of an imaginary vertical line. For example, one small dark object can balance two larger lighter objects.

Radial Balance

In a composition with radial balance, all objects radiate out from a center point in a circular manner. A spiral can be considered to have radial balance as well.

HARMONY

A consistent arrangement of the elements in a composition forms a visual connection between the elements. A recurring similarity in the elements is used: recurring line, value, color, shape, texture, or direction.

Repetition

Repeat some visual element—such as shape, color, or direction—with variations.

Rhythm

Rhythm is the orderly repetition of elements in a pattern to create movement. Elements that are evenly spaced are sedate or formal and can be monotonous. Spacing the elements irregularly creates excitement and interest.

Proximity

Placing elements close together is a simple way to make separate elements look as though they belong together.

VARIETY

Introduce change, diversity, or dynamic tension to the recurring elements of harmony. A recurring difference in the elements can be used: differing line, value, color, shape, texture, or direction. Harmony without variety can be uninteresting, but too much variety can destroy unity and create chaos and confusion.

EMPHASIS

Emphasis involves the creation of a focal point through contrast in value, color, or size. Emphasis usually interrupts the movement of the viewer's eye. It is used to call attention to something and to hold the viewer's interest.

MOVEMENT

The illusion of motion can be created with a visual path between similar elements based on repeated shapes, textures, or values.

PROPORTION

Proportion is the relative relationship of an element measured against the other elements, including dark values to light values, large shapes to small shapes, rough textures to smooth textures, positive to negative space, and so on. Proportion is closely tied to emphasis and focal point.

SPACE

You can create an illusion of depth and volume by paying attention to the relative sizes of the elements, by overlapping elements, and by using perspective, transparency, enclosure, and diminishing detail. Space can be an illusion that causes the viewer to forget the flatness of the picture.

NEGATIVE SPACE

The space around an object is just as important as the object itself. Work for a balance between the positive space (the object) and the negative space (the background) around it. Shapes can be formed in the spaces between, among, and around objects. One artist who uses negative space well is M.C. Escher.

◼ TIP

Many people fear drawing because they've been told or have come to think that they can't draw. This belief can be discouraging and can cause a person to give up in defeat.

Almost anyone can learn to draw at any age. Two basic components make up skill in drawing—development of observational skills and lots of practice. You wouldn't expect to sit down at a piano and play a Bach concerto your first time out. You would need to practice that particular concerto for months to be able to play it reasonably well.

Drawing is a learned skill, not unlike playing a musical instrument, and the amount of effort and time you devote to practice is directly proportional to the results. You cannot draw what you do not notice—focus on the details of the object to be drawn. Observe the edges, the proportions, and the relationships between shapes.

Above all, put in the time. Your work will improve, and you will gain confidence.

"So paint as much as you can. Paint all that you can without fear of painting badly." –CLAUDE MONET

EXERCISE ONE: Word Play

Supplies Needed:

- Sketchbook or journal
- Drawing pencil
- Eraser
- Small slips of paper

1. Write the following words on small slips of paper and toss the slips in a basket.

WORDS: leap, sing, follow, dream, wonder, imagine, freedom, courage, grow, dance, enjoy, laugh, create, believe, breathe, whisper, giggle, shout, twirl, switch, play, flutter, quiet, silence, pause, wait, sigh, shimmy, wisdom, strength, float, push, tickle, twist, shake, glimmer, release, collect, hold, whimsy, hope

2. Choose 1 slip from the basket and do 3 quick thumbnail sketches based on your impression of the word. Do not think, ponder, or agonize—just sketch. If you are not happy with the first 3 sketches, do 3 more. Label your sketches.

3. Choose another word and repeat the exercise. Consider the best sketches for future compositions.

EXERCISE TWO: Patterns and Balance

Supplies Needed:

- Sketchbook or journal
- Drawing pencil
- Eraser

1. Draw 1 simple shape multiple times to create a repetitive pattern.

2. Repeat, except pay more attention to the negative space between the shapes.

3. Using at least 3 shapes (the same or different), draw a symmetrically balanced composition. Repeat for a nearly symmetrically balanced composition, for an asymmetrically balanced composition, and again for a radially balanced composition.

EXERCISE THREE: Contour Line Drawing

Supplies Needed:

- Sketchbook or journal
- Drawing pencil
- Eraser
- A simple object, as described in Step 1

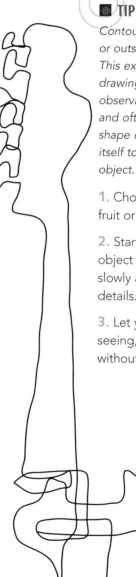

TIP

Contour line drawing is drawing the outline or outside edge (the contour) of an object. This exercise isn't about creating a perfect drawing; it's about developing the skill of observation. The end result is unimportant and often bears little resemblance to the shape of the object. Simply expect the line itself to look like the actual edge of the object.

1. Choose a simple object like a piece of fruit or a small office tool or kitchen tool.

2. Start at any point on the edge of the object and follow the edge with your eyes, slowly and carefully observing all the details.

3. Let your hand draw the shape you are seeing, without lifting your pencil and without looking at your paper.

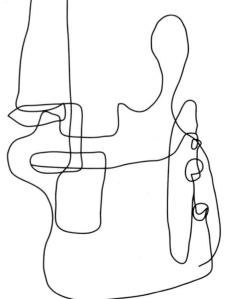

An example of a contour line drawing

References for Further Exploration

WEBSITES OF QUILT ARTISTS

These quilt artists work in series.

Laura Cater-Woods http://www.artquilter.net/

Carol Anne Grotrian http://www.carolannegrotrian.com/

Amanda Perkins
http://www.amandasartquilts.homestead.com/

Barbara S. Randall http://www.cajunbluesstudios.com/

Alison Schwabe http://www.alisonschwabe.com/

Carol Taylor http://www.caroltaylorquilts.com/

The best art quilt website and Internet mailing list is
http://www.quiltart.com/

BOOKS

Atkinson, Jennifer L. *Collage Art: A Step-by-Step Guide & Showcase.* Rockport Publishers: Gloucester, MA, 1999.

Eichorn, Rosemary. *The Art of Fabric Collage: An Easy Introduction to Creative Sewing.* Taunton Press: Newtown, CT, 2003.

Johnston, Ann. *The Quilter's Book of Design.* Quilt Digest Press: Chicago, 2000.

Reflective Queries and Thinking Exercises

- What will your focus or unifying theme be? Why did you select it?

- Take some time and really look at the things around you. For example, if you have a lot of refrigerator magnets, look at their composition on the fridge. Look at the negative space between them.

- Go outside and sit or lie on the lawn. Look at all the shades of color in the trees. Choose one tree and look at the shapes of the leaves, look at the negative space between the leaves and branches. Walk around the tree and look at it from another direction.

Chapter 1 Homework

We are asking you to treat each chapter in this book as a lesson. Each chapter will end with a homework assignment. The goal of these assignments is to have you work on a series of art quilts (9″ × 12″, vertical) developed around a theme and exploring the various techniques found in this book. (See How to Use This Book, page 5.)

Select a theme for your series.

COLOR USE, PERSPECTIVE, AND BORDER OPTIONS

This chapter's lesson covers the use of color and simple perspective, as well as options for bordering your quilt.

"Color is my day-long obsession, joy, and torment." —CLAUDE MONET

color, *n.* The appearance of objects (or light sources) described in terms of a person's perception of their hue, lightness (or brightness), and saturation (from Latin *color*: color).

Sabal Palmettos, by Elin Waterston

Color

Color might be the most powerful tool you as an artist have at your disposal. It can be used to affect emotion, create any mood, or help communicate an idea.

THE VOCABULARY OF COLOR

Primary colors

Secondary colors

Tertiary colors

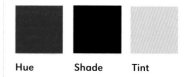

Hue   Shade   Tint

There are three *primary* colors: red, yellow, and blue. The combination of two primary colors results in a *secondary* color: orange, green, or violet. Combining a primary and a secondary color yields a *tertiary* color: red-orange, yellow-orange, yellow-green, blue-green, blue-violet, or red-violet. *Hue* is another word for the name of a color. Color is described in terms of *value*, which is the lightness or darkness of a color, and *saturation*, also known as intensity, which is the degree to which colors have been diluted. The addition of black to a hue results in a *shade*. The addition of white to a hue results in a *tint*.

COLOR TEMPERATURE

Rendez-vous (red), **by Elin Waterston (composition using warm colors)**

Colors are often referred to as warm or cool. The temperature of a color is a result of the wavelength of light reflected from a color. Warm colors are those in the red, orange, and yellow families; these colors are often associated with fire. Cool colors are in the blue, green, and purple families; these are the colors of water. The temperature of a color depends on what other colors are used with it and on the light in which it is viewed.

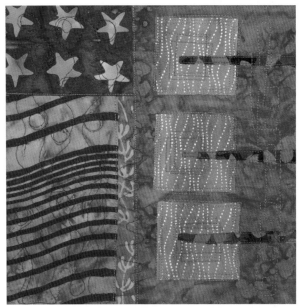

Rendez-vous (blue), **by Elin Waterston (composition using cool colors)**

COLOR AND ITS MOODS

Low-contrast composition—calm   **High-contrast composition—energetic**

Color is both simple and complex. It affects us emotionally and can be used to express or evoke specific emotional responses. Hues in the red and yellow areas of the color wheel are associated with warmth and energy; hues in the blue and green ranges are associated with coolness and calmness. Red can be powerful, exciting, daring, and passionate, but a tint or shade of red (pale pink or deep burgundy) will generate a different response. No two people see color in the same way, and very slight differences in color can produce very different responses.

Color can have different meanings in different cultures. For example, in many Eastern cultures, white is the color of mourning, whereas in many Western cultures, black is the color of mourning. It is important to be sensitive to these cultural differences if your art is depicting or referencing another culture. Also, be aware that people of other backgrounds and cultures may respond to your color choices differently than you intended.

Color can be used representationally or *locally*; that is, you can use the actual color under average lighting conditions—for example, by depicting an apple as red. Color can also be used symbolically or *expressionistically*; that is, you can change the color of an object or scene to express an emotion.

A CONTROLLED COLOR PALETTE

Inflorescence I, **by Jane Dávila**

Inflorescence II, **by Jane Dávila**

Inflorescence III, **by Jane Dávila**

One of the easiest ways to create unity in a series of quilts is to use a controlled color palette. If you use a set group of colors, your quilts will automatically be tied together visually, and the impact of your subject or subjects can be stronger. This is most easily accomplished by picking a stack of fabrics and keeping them out for use and for reference. If the quilts in your series are made from these fabrics and fabrics that go with these, plus an occasional deviant color, the quilts in the series will play well together and the series will be more cohesive. You don't have to use a controlled color palette, but it is one more decision in the process.

Perspective

Perspective is a two-dimensional illusion of a three-dimensional subject or space. *Technical,* or *mechanical,* perspective is based on drawing systems and geometry and includes such principles as vanishing points and gridded planes. *Simple,* or *freehand,* perspective is more intuitive and is based on perception and observation of forms in space.

TECHNICAL PERSPECTIVE

An understanding of the principles of technical perspective can be a valuable asset to any artist, but it's a complicated subject. Whole books have been written on this topic alone. We encourage you to research and explore the subject on your own.

SIMPLE PERSPECTIVE

Simple perspective is more easily translated into fabric, and its use can be very effective. You can achieve the illusion of depth and volume by using the following devices. Combining these devices can give a stronger illusion of depth and encourage viewers to forget that they are seeing a flat picture.

Value

Perspective created using value

Light colors on a dark background will advance. Darker colors define shadows, and lighter colors define areas in light.

Temperature

Perspective created using temperature

Warm colors generally come forward, and cool colors recede slightly. Cool colors define shadows, and warm colors define areas in light. Distant objects appear bluish.

Intensity

Perspective created using intensity

More saturated colors advance and define areas in light; dulled colors recede and define areas in shadow. The farther away an object is, the less colorful it becomes.

Texture

Perspective created using texture

Greater, more definite texture advances and defines areas in light; reduced texture recedes and defines areas in shadow.

Relative Size

Perspective created using relative size

Larger objects appear closer, and smaller objects appear farther away.

Overlapping

Perspective created using overlapping

If one object covers a part of a second object, then the first object appears closer.

Diminishing Detail

Perspective created using diminishing detail

Close objects appear sharp and clearly defined, and objects farther away appear blurred, lacking in detail, and less distinct.

Framing Your Composition

Quilts traditionally have borders that frame the composition, containing the subject. A border can serve the same purpose served by a mat on a print, or a frame on a painting. A border (or frame) around the perimeter visually turns the eye inward, creating a closed form, a complete scene. An open form is a partial glimpse of a portion of a scene that continues beyond the format. A closed form is more formal and structured, and an open form creates a casual, momentary feeling.

BORDER ALTERNATIVES
No Border

In this case the binding or other finished edge will be the "border" (closed form).

Varying Borders

Make the borders different widths or colors on each side to help balance or emphasize the weight or focus of your composition (closed form).

Interrupting Border

An interrupting border cuts off part of the subject and appears to overlap the interior (open form).

Accent Strip

An accent strip, or folded "fillet," can be added between the interior of the quilt and the border or binding for a pop of color on one or more sides. Generally, only ¼″ of the strip shows (on all four sides—closed form; on fewer than four sides—open form).

Curved Border

Topstitch or piece a curved border on one or more sides (open or closed form, depending on the color and number of sides).

Off-Kilter Border

Square the completed quilt top so that the edges are not parallel to any seam (closed form).

◼ HOW TO MAKE A FILLET

Cut a strip of fabric 1″ wide by the length of one side of your quilt. Iron the strip in half, right sides out, so that it now measures ½″ wide. Pin the raw edges of the fillet to the raw edge of one side of the quilt. Repeat, if desired, on all four sides of the quilt. Baste the strips in place by hand or machine. When you add borders or a binding, the fillet will remain in place, with the folded edge toward the inside of the quilt.

Press fillet strip in half.

Pin the fillet to the raw edge of the quilt.

Breaking the Border

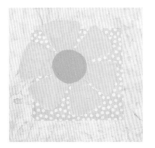

You can create interest by overlapping some design elements with the border on one or more sides. Elements can also overlap or underlap multiple borders. A small contrasting colored strip can be placed within a composition along two or more sides to give the suggestion of a "floating" border.

EXERCISE ONE: Word Play

Paint chips cut into separate squares

Supplies Needed:

- Many different solid or solid-like fabrics or paint chips cut into approximately 1˝ squares
- Sketchbook or journal
- Gluestick
- Pencil
- Small slips of paper

1. Write the following words on small slips of paper and toss the slips in a basket.

WORDS: tropical, classic, romantic, vital, earthy, friendly, soft, welcoming, powerful, rich, regal, magical, nostalgic, energetic, pale, moving, dependable, calm, warm, cool, light, subdued, professional, elegant, hot, cold, fresh, traditional, refreshing, dark, bright, trendy

2. Randomly choose a word from the basket. Using 1˝ squares of fabric or paint chips, create a color combination using 3 different colors in response to the chosen word. Glue this combination into your journal and label it with that word.

3. Repeat with another word.

4. Variations to try with either method: create a color combination using 3 different colors in response to a piece of music (rap, blues, classical, country, pop, swing, and so on).

EXERCISE TWO:
Warm and Cool Combinations

Supplies Needed:

- Many different solid or solid-like fabrics or paint chips cut into approximately 1˝ squares
- Sketchbook or journal
- Gluestick
- Pencil

1. Using 1˝ squares of fabric or paint chips, create a color combination using 4 warm colors.

2. Create a color combination using 4 cool colors.

3. Create a color combination using 3 warm colors and 1 cool color.

4. Create a color combination using 3 cool colors and 1 warm color. Glue these combinations into your journal and label them with their description.

Simple Perspective

Supplies Needed:

- Sketchbook or journal
- Drawing pencil
- Eraser

1. Draw a composition illustrating perspective using relative size.

2. Draw a composition illustrating perspective using overlapping.

3. Draw a composition illustrating perspective using diminishing detail.

4. Draw a composition illustrating perspective using any combination of two or more devices.

References for Further Exploration

WEBSITES OF QUILT ARTISTS

These quilt artists work well with color, use open or closed forms, or use innovative border techniques.

Liz Berg http://www.lizbergartquilts.com/

Karen Eckmeier http://www.quilted-lizard.com/

Gabrielle Swain http://www.gabrielleswain.com/

Laura Wasilowski http://www.artfabrik.com/

BOOKS

Moran, Freddy. *Freddy's House: Brilliant Color in Quilts*. C&T Publishing: Lafayette, CA, 2001.

Wolfrom, Joen. *Color Play: Easy Steps to Imaginative Color in Quilts*. C&T Publishing: Lafayette, CA, 2001.

Reflective Queries and Thinking Exercises

- Will there be a controlled color palette for your series? What will it be? How did you choose it?

- Look for examples of color used to evoke emotions in advertising (print and television).

- Look at some of the quilts you've already made. Think about the bordering options discussed in this chapter. How would applying some of these ideas affect your quilts?

Artists to Study

These artists' works reflect some of the concepts discussed in this chapter.

Wolf Kahn	Paul Klee	Georgia O'Keeffe	Rufino Tamayo
Alain Bordier	Fernando Botero	Paul Gauguin	

Chapter 2 Homework

Start the first quilt in your series, incorporating any part of this chapter's lesson. Remember that all your quilts will be 9˝ × 12˝ in a vertical orientation. Decide whether you will have a controlled color palette for your series.

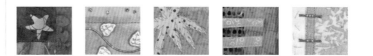

INSPIRATION FROM IMAGES

This chapter's lesson covers the use of photography in quilt design, computer manipulation, images as inspiration, and drawing from a photograph.

"What I wish to show when I paint is the way I see things with my eyes and my heart." —RAOUL DUFY

image, *n.* A reproduction of the form of a person or object (from Latin *imago,* from the root *imitari*: to imitate).

Woodstock Idyll, **by Jane Dávila (quilt made with a photo printed on to fabric)**

Photography in Quilt Design

Photographic imagery is a great source of design inspiration. The photo you choose as your inspiration will depend on what you're trying to say with your piece as well as on the methods you choose to execute your design. A photograph printed directly onto fabric can be incorporated into a quilt, a realistic representation of a photo can be created by way of appliqué or collage, or the image can provide the inspiration in a looser, more abstract way—for example, you could use the color palette from a photo or depict the subject in a nonrepresentational manner.

In general, when working from a photograph, select one with good composition, color, and contrast. Remember that any photo you choose is just a starting point and can be modified in whatever way best serves your design.

Selection of photographs

Using Your Computer

When you use photographs or other images as elements of your quilt design, use either your own photos, photos that you have permission to use, or photos or images that are copyright-free. Search the Internet to find sites where you can download copyright-free photos or illustrations.

Original photo of Sally the cat

Cat photo cropped and manipulated in Photoshop

Toward Femininity, by Elin Waterston (quilt made with a copyright-free image)

Red Cat, by Elin Waterston

PHOTO EDITING

Some image-editing programs, such as Adobe Photoshop and Adobe Photoshop Elements, allow you to manipulate photographs or images. Before purchasing any of these programs, check your digital camera, scanner, and printer to see whether they have any editing capabilities. The kind of image-editing software you choose will depend on the level of manipulation you plan to do—from correcting red eye to making elaborate photo montages.

Before using these programs, you have to get the image into the computer. You can do this by scanning the photo or negative or by uploading an image directly from a digital camera. You can also have your photos put onto compact discs when you have them developed and then upload them from the discs onto your computer.

Once the photo is in the program, you can correct common problems such as red eye and you can adjust the brightness, contrast, and framing. You can correct color or retouch and restore damaged photos. You can also be creative and manipulate the images by playing with color saturation and balance, using special-effects filters, simulating painting techniques, or combining elements to make photo collages.

PRINTING ON FABRIC

Once you've uploaded and adjusted your photos, they can be printed onto fabric using an inkjet printer. You can either use a pretreated fabric or treat fabric yourself. Experiment with your computer and printer settings to see what will give you the best results, and follow the directions specific to the product you're using. The paper trays of standard printers are 8½″ wide, but larger-format printers that allow for a greater printable area are available. Some software programs, as well as printers, have a banner- or panoramic-size page setting, which lets you print longer than standard lengths. Check the page setup in the program you're using, and your printer's features, for specific print-size capabilities.

Commercially Prepared Products

There are several brands of pretreated photo-transfer fabric. Since stock and technology change constantly, check with your local quilt shop for availability and pricing.

Doña Armida, by Jane Dávila (quilt made with a photo transferred onto pretreated fabric)

Do It Yourself

If you wish to keep costs to a minimum, or prefer a softer hand and more control, and don't mind the advance preparation necessary, you can treat fabric yourself with Bubble Jet Set, a product designed to bond dyes to natural fibers (specifically cotton and silk). Although starting with white fabric will yield the most accurate colors, consider experimenting with colored or printed fabrics as a base. Detailed directions for the use of Bubble Jet Set can be found on the bottle.

There are currently printers and inks that allow you to print directly onto untreated fabric. Simply back pieces of prewashed cotton fabric with freezer paper, trim them, and print. Because technology is changing all the time, doing some research on current inks and printers before proceeding is worthwhile.

Mind & Memory (Ansonia), by Elin Waterston (quilt made with a photo printed onto fabric)

Photographs as Inspiration

You might choose to use a photograph as a starting point without depicting the entire image. One way to do this is to use isolated pieces of the image instead of the whole image. Cropping out portions of the photo can enhance or emphasize the details you wish to portray.

To help define a composition, create a viewfinder by cutting two L-shaped pieces of cardboard or heavy paper. Place the viewfinder pieces over your photo and adjust the opening until you find a composition that you like. You can place the main elements of your photo centrally so that the image is completely contained within the viewfinder, or you can crop the image so that some elements are only partially within the frame. You can also crop the image to frame it either horizontally or vertically. Choose a layout that reflects the way you wish to portray your subject.

Seagull photograph

Composition option 1—eliminating extraneous elements

Composition option 2—emphasizing the horizontal

Composition option 3—emphasizing the vertical

Another way to use a photo as inspiration is to abstract the image. Rather than rendering the subject in a figuratively representational sense, you can reduce it to simple lines and forms, or choose certain design elements from the image and stylize or exaggerate them.

Daylily photo

Daylily sketch 1—detailed

Daylily sketch 2—less detail

Daylily sketch 3—simple lines

Daylily sketch 4—stylized and abstract

Daylily finished quilt, by Elin Waterston

Art as Inspiration

Children's art, fine art, folk art, and mosaics can all serve as inspiration when designing an art quilt, but you must be careful not to copy anything directly without permission, because doing so is a copyright infringement. Interpreting someone else's art into another medium does not create an original work. You can, however, be inspired by the colors and forms in a work of art and use this inspiration as a starting point for your own design, or to pay homage to an artist or artwork in your own style. Besides, the point in becoming an artist is to express yourself, not someone else!

Ashanti fertility statue

Asante Abusua, **by Jane Dávila**

Drawing From a Photo

When designing a fabric collage quilt based on a photograph, select one with a simple composition and easily identifiable shadows and highlights. A photo with a complex composition and too much detail will be difficult to break down into the enclosed shapes needed for a fabric collage. As you gain more experience with drawing from photos, you can move on to more complex compositions.

Many people find drawing intimidating. Although it's a skill that takes time to perfect, it's a skill that can be learned. Training yourself to see the way an artist sees is important. Look at things in terms of shapes, lines, and spatial relationships. Take a sketch pad with you everywhere you go and practice, practice, practice.

Complex composition, too much detail—poor choice

Simple composition, clear shadows and highlights—good choice

◼ A WORD ABOUT TRACING

Although tracing might make copying a photograph easier, ultimately the drawbacks of tracing far outweigh the benefits. Relying on tracing will limit your subject options (after all, how does one trace a live model?); your ability to manipulate size, scale, and proportion; and your ability to edit your composition. Tracing is a crutch that prevents you from learning the proper way to draw freehand. However, tracing is appropriate on some occasions, such as when you trace a sketch that you have drawn freehand to make it into a pattern for an art quilt, or when you trace a photo for practice or to get a better sense of shapes, scale, or proportion.

Original photo

Rough sketch

Detailed sketch

Shaded sketch

Linear drawing of enclosed shapes

Fabric options

When you begin to draw from a photo, start out by "blocking in" the shapes: that is, reducing all the elements in the image to basic shapes. Be careful to check the proportions and relative placement of the elements of your subject. How much space separates them? Are the shapes touching or overlapping each other?

After all the basic shapes are drawn, begin to fine-tune your drawing by adding some details. You may find that you need to do several sketches before you feel you've captured the essence of your subject. Once you have a rough sketch you're happy with, add the range of values from light to dark of your subject by shading with your pencil. Shading will give your sketch three-dimensionality and will help describe its form.

To turn this drawing into fabric art, you must enclose all the shapes, so they can be cut out. Make a linear drawing of the highlights, mid-tones, and shadows (do this by placing tracing paper over your sketch so you retain the integrity of the original), clearly marking what's what, to create a map to follow when you start to lay out the fabric pieces.

When selecting fabric for your collage, look carefully at the colors in your photograph. Remember to let yourself see the true colors, and not what you *think* is correct (white is rarely white, and black is rarely black). Be sure you have enough variety. For instance, if you break down your sketch into highlight, light medium, dark medium, and dark, then you must have four different fabrics. Your use of color should be determined by the subject itself, how you see your subject, and how you want to describe it. Choose your fabric colors carefully, and determine whether solid colors, prints, or a combination will best serve your design.

Two Pumpkins, **by Elin Waterston**

"Drawing is not following a line on the model; it is drawing your sense of the thing." –ROBERT HENRI

EXERCISE ONE:

Working From a Pattern— Pear Quilt

Supplies Needed:

- Pear pattern (page 32)
- Tracing paper
- Fine marker (Sharpie or Identipen)
- ¼ yard of fusible web
- ⅛ yard or large scraps of 6 fabrics: highlight, light medium, dark medium, dark, stem, and shadow
- Iron
- Scissors
- Pins
- Background fabric, approximately 11″ × 15″
- Coordinating threads
- Stabilizer
- Optional border fabric
- Batting
- Backing

Original photo

1. Trace the pear pattern onto tracing paper using a fine marker. Number, or otherwise label, each element.

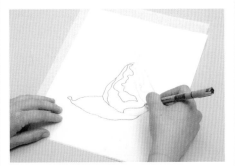

Pear pattern drawn on tracing paper

2. Write a word on the top of the tracing paper so you don't inadvertently reverse the elements once you start the process of transferring everything to fabric.

3. From the back of the traced image, copy the pattern elements (in pencil) onto the paper side of a piece of fusible web, leaving about ¼″ between the elements.

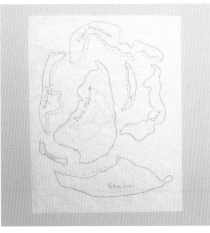

Pattern pieces drawn on fusible web

4. Label each element to correspond with the numbers on the tracing paper pattern.

5. Make sure to mark any areas where fabric pieces will underlap other elements, using a dotted line. Determine areas of overlap by deciding which pieces are farthest from the viewer's eye. Any elements that are in the background will go underneath elements in the foreground.

6. Roughly cut apart the fusible web pieces.

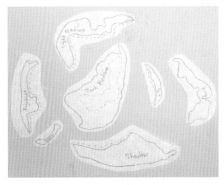

Pattern pieces cut roughly apart

7. Fuse these pieces to the wrong side of their corresponding fabrics (highlight, light medium, dark medium, dark, stem, and shadow).

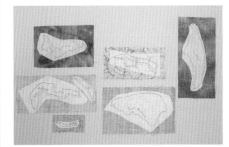

Pattern pieces fused to the wrong side of selected fabrics

8. Cut out all the fabric pieces, allowing a little extra around areas marked for underlapping, as determined in Step 5.

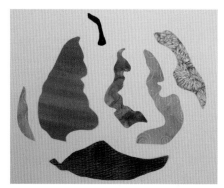

Fused fabric cut out

9. Pin the tracing paper drawing to the right side of the background fabric.

10. Peel off the fusible backing paper and place all the elements on the background fabric, sliding them underneath the tracing paper drawing. Start with elements that will be overlapped by others (for example, the shadow should be placed in position before the pear pieces), using the tracing paper drawing as a map.

Pieces placed on background fabric, using tracing paper map for positioning

11. Once all the pieces are in place, carefully lift up the paper map to check that the placement looks correct and that there are no areas of background showing through among the pear pieces.

12. Fuse everything in place by ironing with a hot, dry iron for 15–20 seconds, or until the pieces are secure.

Pieces fused in place on background fabric

13. Square up the background fabric and add borders, if desired.

With borders added

Pear pattern. Key: H = highlight; LM = light medium; DM = dark medium; D = dark; ST = stem; SH = shadow

14. You have 2 options for finishing your quilt:

Option 1—Stitch the pieces in place using coordinating threads with stabilizer underneath; then layer, baste, and quilt.

Option 2—Layer and baste; then stitch the pieces in place with free-motion quilting.

Finished *Pear quilt*, by Elin Waterston

EXERCISE TWO:
Working From an Original Drawing

Supplies Needed:

- Original photo
- Tracing paper
- Sketchbook
- Drawing pencil
- Fine marker—Sharpie or Identipen
- Fusible web
- Fabrics to match the elements of the photo
- Iron
- Scissors
- Background fabric, at least 6″ larger than your subject
- Stabilizer
- Coordinating threads
- Optional border fabric
- Batting
- Backing

Original photo

1. Choose a photo that has clear shadows and highlights and is not too detailed.

2. Identify the highlight and shadow areas—the planes of lights, mediums, and darks. Following the instructions in Drawing from a Photo (page 29), create a sketch of your photo.

Drawing made from the original photo

3. Trace your sketch onto tracing paper, breaking it down into lights, mediums, and darks, and noting where fabric will need to underlap or overlap other pieces. Remember that each shape must be enclosed so you can cut it out of fabric.

4. Label every shape.

5. Write a word on the top of the tracing paper so you don't inadvertently reverse the elements once you start the process of transferring everything to fabric.

6. Turn the tracing paper over. From the back of the traced image, copy the pattern elements (in pencil) onto the paper side of a piece of fusible web, leaving about ¼″ between the elements.

7. Add extra around any areas that will underlap another shape.

8. Cut roughly around each shape.

9. Using a hot, dry iron, fuse each element to the wrong side of the selected fabrics.

10. Cut out all the fabric pieces, allowing a little extra around areas marked for underlapping.

11. Peel off the backing and iron the pieces onto a generously sized piece of background fabric, using the tracing paper copy as a map (as described above). Remember not to iron any pieces in place until all the elements are placed on your background fabric.

12. Square up the quilt and add borders, if desired.

13. Finishing options are the same as those described in Exercise 1.

Alex, Boston, by Elin Waterston

◼ A NOTE ABOUT SHADOWING

Sometimes when you are placing a light-colored fabric on top of a darker fabric (such as the lightest skin tone in Alex, Boston *on the darker blue background), the dark fabric will "shadow" through the light fabric, changing its color. To prevent the shadow effect, cut a ring of fusible web rather than a solid shape for the light fabric. On the fusible web, trace the outside edge of the element and draw a dotted line about* ¼˝ *inside that line. Cut roughly around the solid outside line and exactly on the dotted line. Fuse this ring onto the back of your light fabric and cut around the shape on the solid outside line. You will now have fusible web just on the outside* ¼˝ *of your element. When this piece is fused in place on top of the dark fabric, carefully separate the two fabrics and cut away the underlapping dark fabric.*

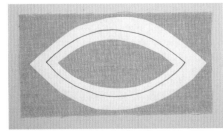

Fused ring on wrong side of fabric

References for Further Exploration

WEBSITES OF QUILT ARTISTS

These quilt artists work with imagery.

Pamela Allen
http://pamelart2.homestead.com/quiltythings.html

Susan Carlson http://www.susancarlson.com/

Janet Ghio http://www.quiltcollage.com/

Lesley Riley http://www.lalasland.com/

IMAGE-EDITING PROGRAMS

Adobe Photoshop www.adobe.com/digitalimag/main.html

Adobe Photoshop Elements
www.abobe.com/support/downloads/main.html

Paint Shop Pro www.jasc.com/products/paintshoppro/

Each image-editing computer program will likely have its own manual or guidebook.

BOOKS

Carlson, Susan, E. *Free-Style Quilts: A "No Rules" Approach.* C&T Publishing: Lafayette, CA, 2000.

Edwards, Betty. *Drawing on the Right Side of the Brain.* 2nd rev. ed. Penguin Putnam, New York, NY, 1999.

Laury, Jean Ray. *Imagery on Fabric: A Complete Surface Design Handbook.* 2nd. ed. C&T Publishing: Lafayette, CA, 1997.

Reflective Queries and Thinking Exercises

- Take some time to do some photography. Spend a day at a zoo or botanical garden and shoot a roll of film or some digital images.

- Do the same with a pencil and a sketch pad. (Maybe not at the zoo—it's hard to get the elephants to stand still while you sketch them.)

- Abstract an image from a photo. Begin drawing the image in its representational form. Take that image through several stages of abstraction, until the subject is barely (or not at all) recognizable.

Artists to Study

These photographers and artists create works that are inspired by imagery or incorporate photographs.

Raoul Dufy	Edward Hopper
Andy Warhol	Henri Cartier-Bresson
Robert Frank	Wayne Thiebaud
David Hockney	Roy Lichtenstein
Walker Evans	Wassily Kandinsky
Constantin Brancusi	Richard Diebenkorn
Willem De Kooning	Piet Mondrian

Chapter 3 Homework

Begin another (9˝ × 12˝, vertical) quilt in your series, using an image as inspiration.

FABRIC COLLAGE

This chapter's lesson covers the basics of fabric collage and appliqué design and techniques.

"Art = a mad search for individualism."—PAUL GAUGUIN

collage, *n.* An artistic composition of materials and objects pasted over a surface (from French *coller*: to glue).

appliqué, *v.* To decorate by cutting pieces of one material and applying them to the surface of another (from French *appliquer*: to apply).

The Basics of Collage and Appliqué Design

A collage can be figurative, representing a person, an animal, or a scene. It can be narrative, telling a story, making a social or political statement, or portraying cultural or historical significance. Or it can be completely abstract and nonrepresentational, emphasizing color, shape, and texture.

A collage can be intricate in detail or simple in its composition. With any of these variations, you achieve your goal by piecing together seemingly random objects and images, creating a cohesive whole. Collage allows you to organize visual elements into a harmonious creation, which can express more as a whole than its individual components can.

Merula #2, **by Elin Waterston**

Theseus & the Minotaur, **by Elin Waterston**

As in other media, any subject matter can be appropriate for collaging—still life, figures, landscapes, and seascapes are all compelling collage subjects.

Collaged compositions often employ the fundamental principles of design—balance, harmony, variety, emphasis, movement, proportion, and space—as well as basic design elements like shape, color, and line.

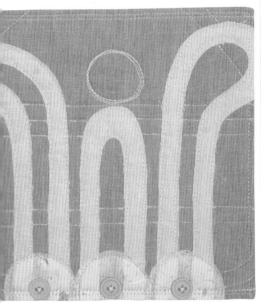

French Horn, by Jane Dávila

STYLISTIC VARIATIONS

There are many approaches to collage design. Whatever approach you take, it's important to create a sense of unity, a sense that all the elements belong together.

Color and Shape Collage

Abstract compositions emphasize the arrangement of colors and shapes. When creating an abstract composition, consider the variety of shapes and colors you incorporate—warm and cool colors, organic and geometric shapes, simple and complex shapes—as well as the negative space that is created by the placement of the elements.

Abstractions 1, **by Elin Waterston**

In any composition, adding one element that differs from the others will make the singular element the focal point. If a composition consists of all cool colors and one warm color is introduced, the warm color becomes the focus.

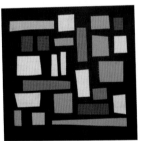

Collage composition using only cool colors

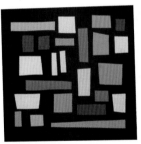

Collage composition using cool colors and a single warm color

Similarly, if all the shapes in a composition are geometric and one organic shape is added, the organic shape takes the focus.

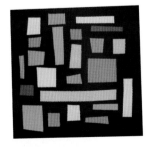

Collage composition using only geometric shapes

Collage composition using geometric shapes and a single organic shape

Collage With a Focus

Some collages contain a central image or focal point—a photograph, an illustration, or a found object—around which the other elements are built. Additional elements can emphasize or accentuate the central image and create an interesting visual arrangement.

Missing Tuss, by Elin Waterston (collage composition using a photograph as a focal point)

DESIGN APPROACHES

When beginning a collage, you might want to plan your design by doing either a detailed drawing or a rough sketch. When working from a drawing or sketch, it's helpful to use a clear acetate or tracing paper overlay as a positioning guide, but be sure to allow yourself some room for change. Don't be afraid to change something from your original sketch if you feel the change improves your composition.

If you prefer to be spontaneous, cut shapes arbitrarily and play with how the juxtapositioning of different shapes changes the dynamics of the composition.

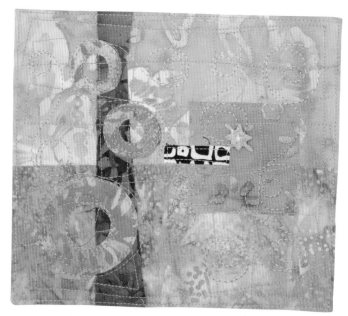

Abstractions 2, by Elin Waterston

Experimentation is a key element of collage! Regardless of the materials you use or the approach you take, spend time arranging and fine-tuning your collage. Many collages that seem to be a haphazard arrangement actually take hours of planning, arranging, rearranging, and tweaking to get that spontaneous look.

 TIP

When trying out composition options, sketch or take digital photos of them. This way you can compare the options, choose the best one, and recreate it.

Attaching the Elements

There are several methods of adhering collage elements to a background. They can be fused, glued, or pinned in place and then secured by stitching through the background and collage elements only, or they can be held in place with quilting after the piece has been layered with batting and backing. If the composition consists of many small pieces, you can place tulle over the entire composition and quilt through all the layers. The tulle will hold the small pieces in place.

"It doesn't make much difference how the paint is put on as long as something has been said. Technique is just a means of arriving at a statement."

—JACKSON POLLOCK

EXERCISE ONE: Color Collage

Supplies Needed:

- 3 pieces of fabric, about 6″ × 6″, with fusible web on the wrong side
- Scissors
- Background fabric, 9″ × 12″
- Iron

1. Cut 3 various organic (but not too representational) shapes out of the prefused fabric.

2. Arrange the shapes on the 9″ × 12″ background fabric.

TIP

Try overlapping the shapes, placing them off to one side or in the center, or so that they touch the outer edge of the background (keeping in mind the seam allowance, if any, needed for edge finishing). Explore the relationship between the shapes. Look carefully at the negative space that is formed by varying the placement of the shapes. Determine what arrangement is the most effective for your design.

Elements balanced and evenly spaced

Elements touching

Elements overlapping

Elements grouped and off-center

3. Reposition the shapes in a different configuration.

4. When you find a composition you like, fuse the pieces in place with a hot, dry iron.

EXERCISE TWO: Collage With a Focus

Supplies Needed:

- Photo transferred to fabric, or an image cut from a novelty fabric
- Fusible web
- Scraps of coordinating or contrasting fabric (prefused)
- Buttons, charms, found objects
- Scissors
- Iron

1. Fuse and crop a photo-transferred or novelty-fabric image.

2. Place it somewhere on the 9″ × 12″ background fabric.

3. Add elements (fused fabric shapes, buttons, charms, found objects, and so on) to the background to emphasize the photo.

4. Move the elements around to find the most aesthetically pleasing and expressive layout.

Composition option 1

Composition option 2

Composition option 3

5. When you are satisfied with the arrangement, fuse or otherwise secure everything in place, or make a note of where things go—sketch or take a digital photo of things that need to be attached later.

Collage with a focus—finished quilt:
Brilliant Anyway, by Elin Waterston

References for Further Exploration

WEBSITES OF ARTISTS

These artists work with collage techniques.

Pamela Allen http://pamelart.homestead.com/titlepage.html

Susan Carlson http://www.susancarlson.com/

Karen Eckmeier http://www.quilted-lizard.com/

Claudine Hellmuth http://www.collageartist.com/

Lesley Riley http://www.lalasland.com/

Joan Schulze http://www.joan-of-arts.com/

BOOKS

Brommer, Gerald F. *Collage Techniques: A Guide for Artists and Illustrators.* Watson-Guptill Publications: New York, 1994.

Carlson, Susan E. *Free-Style Quilts: A "No Rules" Approach.* C&T Publishing: Lafayette, CA, 2000.

Reflective Queries and Thinking Exercises

■ Experiment with different methods of creating a collage composition and try to determine what the most appropriate procedures are for you—careful planning of the composition, haphazardly arranging elements, or something in between.

■ How does changing the positioning of collage elements affect the work? What kinds of compositions are the most visually stimulating, emotionally effective, or aesthetically pleasing?

Artists to Study

These artists use collage techniques in their work.

Henri Matisse (late works)	Hans Arp	Kurt Schwitters
David Hockney	Jasper Johns	Man Ray
Robert Motherwell	Romare Bearden	Arthur Dove	Max Ernst

Chapter 4 Homework

Start a new quilt (9″ × 12″, vertical) employing some of the collage principles and techniques discussed in this chapter.

INNOVATIVE PIECING

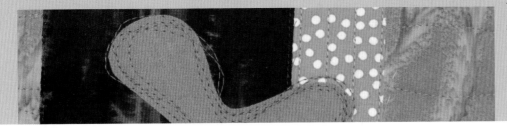

This chapter's lesson covers several unusual machine-piecing techniques.

"Artists who seek perfection in everything achieve it in nothing." —EUGÈNE DELACROIX

piecing, *v.* To repair, renew, or complete by adding pieces; to join into a whole (from Middle English *pece*: piece).

Piecing Techniques

Numerous piecing techniques are available for you to use. Covered here are a few of the more unusual ones that are most readily adaptable to art quilting. Piecing can be the ultimate result of a work, or you can use the techniques to create a background piece on which to place appliquéd or collaged subjects, or you can use piecing in combination with other techniques. In general, it is best to work bigger than you would like your piece to finish, and then trim to size—unless you are working on a precisely drafted design.

MACHINE-PIECED FREEHAND CURVES

Playa de Paracas, by Jane Dávila

Folklórico, by Jane Dávila

Machine piecing freehand curves is a wonderful no-template way of incorporating curves into your piece or border. This technique works best with easy, gentle curves, which are cut freehand through layered fabric. Registration marks are used to ensure that your piece is flat when it's finished. Every curve is different, and the effect is casual and dynamic. This technique can be successfully employed when you want to depict a landscape, or when an organic effect is desired. Use the technique for both figurative and abstract works.

WONKY PIECING

Impromptu, by Jane Dávila

Wonky piecing is another spontaneous technique, and it employs rotary cutting and straight-line sewing to achieve a delightfully whimsical effect. The technique requires a little planning to ensure that you are always sewing a straight line, but it can be liberating and fun. This technique is used with figurative subjects as well as abstract designs, but it also works with geometric shapes like traditional quilt blocks.

INSERT STRIPS

Blue Aspens, by Elin Waterston

The insert strips technique introduces the unexpected into the expected, and can help create a focal point or direction of interest. A solid, pieced, or appliquéd background is sliced, and strips of a contrasting color are inserted into the openings. These strips create movement in your piece. Use this technique to create effective, interesting backgrounds on which to place other elements.

"Technique does not exist in itself, it is only the substance of the creative machinery." —ANSEL ADAMS

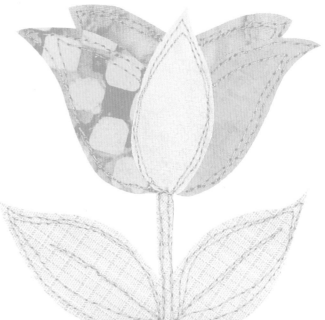

EXERCISE ONE: Freehand Curves

Supplies Needed:

- 2 squares of fabric, 9″ × 9″
- Rotary cutter and mat
- Pencil, in a color to contrast with your fabrics
- Fine pins

1. Place a 9″ square of fabric right side up on the cutting mat.

Start with fabric right side up.

2. Place a second 9″ square of fabric right side up on top of the first, leaving about 3″ of the first square showing on the left side.

Remember that both fabrics must be right side up.

3. With a rotary cutter, cut a long, gentle freehand curve away from you close to the left edge of the top fabric.

Keep the curve simple and loose.

4. Remove the small slice of the top fabric and the right side of the bottom fabric.

The pieces will fit together perfectly.

5. Turn the 2 remaining pieces of fabric wrong sides up and carefully line up the curved edges.

Be careful with the bias edges!

6. Draw registration marks on the edges every 1″–2″, perpendicular to the cut edges.

Draw small marks with a contrasting-colored pencil.

7. Place the fabric pieces right sides together, matching the first set of registration marks, and pin at the marks.

Carefully line up each set of registration marks.

8. Pin again at the next set of marks and then carefully pin between the marks, about every ½″. Pin very close to the edge to allow the fabric to bend.

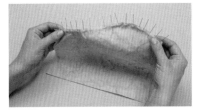

Very fine pins will make this part easier.

9. Sew the pieces together using an ⅛″ seam allowance, removing pins as you come to them. (Contrasting thread shown for visibility.)

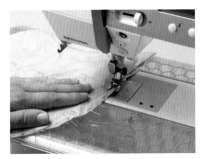

Only worry about the part going through the machine; the rest of the piece will not lie flat. Flatten each section as you approach it.

10. Press the piece from the back. Add another curved seam in the same manner, if desired.

Press the seam in whichever direction lies flatter.

EXERCISE TWO:
Wonky Piecing

We've chosen a Log Cabin block for this exercise. Feel free to experiment with other forms on your own.

Supplies Needed:

- Fabric for a center, 5½″ × 5½″
- Rotary cutter, mat, and ruler
- 2 strips 2″ wide of each of 3–4 different fabrics

1. Cut at least 2 sides of the center square at a slight angle.

Trim center square.

2. Sew 1 strip to 1 side of the center square, keeping the raw edges even.

Add first strip.

3. Press the seam away from the center square. Trim the ends of the strip and then trim the newly added strip at a slight angle, not parallel to the sewing line.

Trim the right edge even with the center square.

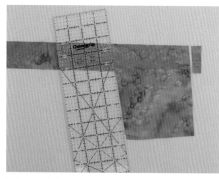

Trim the left edge even with the center square.

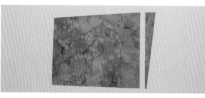

Cut the new strip at a slight angle.

4. Continue adding strips 1 at a time to the other 3 sides of the center in a clockwise direction. After adding each piece, trim the ends even and then trim the newly added strip at a slight angle, not parallel to the sewing line.

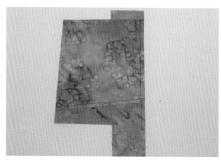

Add another strip to the unit.

Trim the new strip even with the center unit on the right and left sides.

Cut the new strip on a slight angle prior to adding the next strip to the center unit.

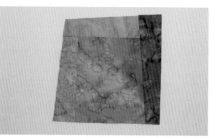

Center unit with one strip added to each side.

5. Continue adding strips, trimming and cutting at an angle until you have 3 strips around the center on all 4 sides.

Center with three strips added to each side.

6. Square up the block.

Insert Strips

METHOD ONE

Supplies Needed:

- Background fabric, 10˝ × 10˝
- Rotary cutter, mat, and ruler
- 1˝ strips of accent fabric

1. With a ruler and a rotary cutter, cut across the background square from side to side in any direction, at any angle.

Cut across the background square.

 TIP

Audition cuts before making them by laying accent strips across the background fabric until you find an angle that pleases you.

2. Piece a strip of accent fabric between the pieces of the square. Press the seams toward the accent strip.

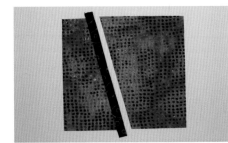

Strip sewn to one side

TIP

Pressing the seams toward the accent strip makes the strips appear to float over the background. Pressing the seams away from the accent strip will give a reverse appliqué effect.

One strip pieced into the background fabric

3. Cut across the accented square, this time in another direction. Piece in another strip of accent fabric.

Cut across the background square and the previous accent strip.

Second strip pieced into the background fabric

4. Continue cutting and piecing until you achieve the desired effect.

Cut across the background again at any angle. You may cut through one or more of the previous accent strips, if desired.

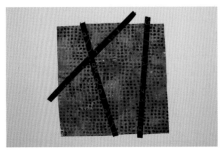

Third strip pieced into the background fabric

5. Square up the block.

Completed piece, Method 1

For another option, consider using more than 1 accent color or varying the finished widths of the insert strips from ½˝ to 1˝ (or more).

METHOD TWO

Supplies Needed:

- Background fabric, 10″ × 10″
- Rotary cutter, mat, and ruler
- 1″ strips of accent fabric
- Iron

1. With a ruler and a rotary cutter, cut across the background square from side to side in any direction, at any angle.

Cut across the background.

2. Set the smaller piece aside and cut the larger piece in the same manner. Continue cutting until you have achieved the desired effect.

Try not to cut too many pieces, or use steep angles the first time you try this method. Using many pieces and steep angles will increase the level of difficulty.

3. Sew a strip of accent fabric between the last 2 pieces cut, pressing the seams toward the insert strip.

First accent strip pieced into the last cut made.

4. Continuing adding strips and sewing in reverse order until you've sewn a strip between the 2 pieces created by the first cut that you made. Press all the seams toward the insert strips.

All accent strips pieced into the background fabric.

 TIP

It may be necessary to trim interior edges after each strip is added.

5. Square up the block.

Completed piece, Method 2

Variations to try with either method: place all the strips going in the same direction; piece the insert strips themselves first; taper the strips as you sew; cut across appliquéd and pieced backgrounds.

References for Further Exploration

WEBSITES OF QUILT ARTISTS

These quilt artists work with interesting piecing techniques.

Cynthia England http://www.englanddesign.com/

Caryl Bryer Fallert http://www.bryerpatch.com/

Ruth McDowell http://www.ruthbmcdowell.com/

Jan Mullen http://www.stargazey.com/

Vikki Pignatelli http://home.att.net/~vikkipm/

Carol Taylor http://www.caroltaylorquilts.com/

BOOKS

Cummings, Sandi. *Thinking Outside the Block: Step by Step to Dynamic Quilts.* C&T Publishing: Lafayette, CA, 2004.

Dunn, Sarah Sacks, ed. *Innovative Piecing.* Rodale Books: Emmaus, PA, 2001.

England, Cynthia. *Picture Piecing.* England Design: Houston, 2002.

Hire, Dianne S. *Quilter's Playtime.* American Quilter's Society: Paducah, KY, 2004.

McDowell, Ruth. *Piecing: Expanding the Basics.* C&T Publishing: Lafayette, CA, 1998.

Mullen, Jan. *Cut Loose the Stargazey Way.* C&T Publishing: Lafayette, CA, 2001.

REFLECTIVE QUERIES AND THINKING EXERCISES

- Look at some of the quilts you've already made. Think about the piecing options discussed in this chapter. How would applying some of these ideas have affected your quilts?

- How would adding a curved border to a geometric quilt affect the overall composition?

Artists to Study

The work of these artists reflects the feeling of the shapes and forms described in this chapter.

Piet Mondrian	Wassily Kandinsky
Josef Albers	Ilya Bolotowsky
Morris Louis	Fernand Léger
Paul Klee	Frank Stella
Theo van Doesburg	Robert Delaunay
Sonia Delaunay	

Chapter 5 Homework

Start a new quilt (9″ × 12″, vertical) employing some innovative piecing techniques.

PAINT EFFECTS

This chapter's lesson covers various techniques for applying paint and foil to fabric.

"Every child is an artist. The problem is how to remain an artist once he grows up." —**PABLO PICASSO**

paint, *n.* A mixture of pigment in liquid form, used as a decorative or protective coating (from Latin *pingere*: to paint).

Still Life with Pears, **by Elin Waterston**

Painting

PAINTS AND BRUSHES

Textile paints are made specifically for fabric painting, and many brands are readily available in numerous colors and types, including opaque (for dark fabrics) and metallics. Acrylic paints can also be used on fabric, but they can affect the hand of the fabric; a textile medium can be added to acrylic paints to soften the hand. Most textile paints need to be heat set—by ironing, once the paint has dried. Acrylic paints are permanent without any heat setting. Each brand and type of paint will have different characteristics, and different fabrics will receive paint differently. It's important to experiment with various paints and fabrics and practice before beginning a project.

Koi Pond, by Elin Waterston (quilt painted with Jacquard Lumiere metallic paints)

Paintbrushes come in many shapes and sizes, with long or short handles, in both synthetic and natural bristles. Your choice of brush is largely a matter of personal preference, and as you gain more painting experience, you'll find what types you're most comfortable with. Ultimately, your design will determine what size and shape brush you need—small rounds or flats for fine details, and large rounds, flats, or filberts for wide strokes or large areas of color.

FABRIC

Natural fibers, such as cotton and silk, work well for fabric painting. The color of the paint will be affected by the color of the fabric. Painting on white fabric will result in pure, accurate colors, and the same color paint will look quite different when applied to colored fabric. Know your color wheel and test pigments to see how they change with the fabric color. That said, painting on colored or printed fabric can yield interesting effects, so experiment with lots of fabric—different colors, solids and prints.

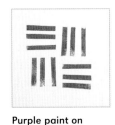 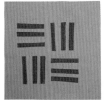

Purple paint on white fabric   **Purple paint on light blue fabric**   **Purple paint on yellow-orange fabric**

Prewash the fabric to remove any sizing, which can repel the pigment. Check to make sure that all the sizing has been removed by dropping a small amount of water onto the fabric—if the water soaks in, the fabric is ready to paint. If the water beads on top of the fabric, you might need to rewash.

When you're ready to begin painting, place the fabric on a protected surface (covered with newsprint, batting, a plastic sheet, or a shower curtain) or stretch the fabric on a frame or in a hoop. Use an inexpensive wooden or plastic hoop, as it's likely to get wet.

Design and Application

Painted designs can be representational (creating a picture) or abstract (creating textures or interesting color compositions). You can use paint to create an image to be the focus of a piece, add detail to appliqué or collage shapes, or create patterned fabric. Pigment can be applied with brushes, sponges, stamps, or textured rollers or it can be spattered, sprayed, or dripped onto fabric. Experiment and use your imagination!

FREEHAND PAINTING

To create a representational design, draw the design lightly on the fabric and paint it in using small brushes. Test the viscosity of the paints on another small piece of your fabric. Fabric can be very absorbent, and you might need to experiment with the amount of water you add to the paint to get the right coverage while avoiding bleeding.

For a more abstract design, apply paint by spattering, dabbing it on with a sponge, or using broad strokes with a wide brush. You can achieve interesting effects by wetting the fabric before applying pigment or by overlapping colors and allowing them to bleed together. Again, test the paints on a separate piece of fabric to determine the correct viscosity.

As with most surface-design techniques, the more you practice, the better you will get. With experience, you will become more comfortable working with paint. You'll gain an understanding of how much pigment you need to load on your brush and what the appropriate viscosity of the pigment is. Be prepared for mistakes and make them work for you!

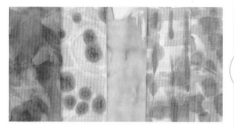

Painted fabric samples

STAMPING

Commercial stamps

There are lots of ready-made stamps on the market that can be used in fabric stamping, or you can make original stamps yourself. Most commercial stamps are copyrighted, so unless you are using them for personal use only, you must check the copyright information and get permission from the manufacturer. If you're uncertain about the copyright status of a stamp, check with the manufacturer.

Handmade stamps

Many people prefer to make their own stamps. Stamps can be carved or cut from linoleum blocks and soft-cut blocks with linoleum-cutting tools. Craft foam, erasers, weather-stripping, and moldable foam can all be used to create stamps. A pattern can be made of string, mounted on a base (like a block of wood), and used to print on fabric. For this kind of block printing, pigment is applied to the block with a brayer and then transferred to the fabric.

◼ TIP

When gluing elements to a mount to create a stamp, be sure to use non-water-soluble glue. You will need to wash the stamp to remove the paint, and you don't want your design to come unglued!

Found stamps

Stamps can also be found. Natural objects like cut vegetables, leaves, or plants and household objects like kitchen utensils or tools can all be used to make interesting prints. Painted patterns and textures can be created using bubble wrap, a block of wood, a rolling pin wrapped with rubber bands, the end of a spool of thread...search your house for potential stamps, and experiment!

Stamped fabrics

Foiling

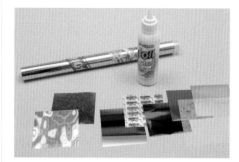

Foiling supplies

Metallic foils are thin layers of foil attached to cellophane sheets, which can be transferred to fabric using liquid glue, fusible web, or bonding powder. You can apply glue by using a spouted bottle or by painting, sponging, or stamping it on in various designs to be foiled. You can cut fusible web into specific shapes or tear it to create organic rough edges, fuse the web onto fabric, and then apply foil to the fused shapes. For a spattered effect, sprinkle bonding powder (powdered fusible web) on the surface of your fabric or quilt top and apply foil to the powder.

Foils come in a wide variety of colors and patterns, including variegated, iridescent, and holographic colors. Foils can add sparkle or highlights to design elements or can be used to create patterns. Different brands of foil will have specific instructions, so be sure to check the package for details about the product you use.

TIP
Once foil has been applied, the quilt should not be washed or ironed directly on the foiled area.

Speak of Africa, by Jane Dávila (quilt with foil applied with fusible web)

EXERCISE ONE:
Abstract Painting

Supplies Needed:

- Prewashed white or colored fabric, or a pieced quilt top

- Acrylic or fabric paints in various colors

- Wide flat or round brushes

- Iron

1. On a protected work surface, paint an abstract design onto a piece of fabric or a pieced quilt top, with diluted acrylic or fabric paint.

Apply diluted paint.

2. Add layers of other colors while the paint is wet or after the first color has dried.

Add layers of other colors.

3. Allow the paint to dry.

4. Heat set the paint by ironing.

Painted fabric

EXERCISE TWO:
Representational Painting

Supplies Needed:

- Prewashed white or light-colored fabric

- Fabric or acrylic paints

- Small flat and round brushes

- Pencil

- Iron

1. Lightly draw a design onto a piece of fabric with a pencil.

2. Using small brushes, paint the design using fabric or acrylic paints.

 TIP

If the paints are too watery, they will bleed. Test the viscosity of the paints on a scrap of fabric.

3. Layer colors and add shading and details.

Paint in the design.

4. Allow the paint to dry.

5. Heat set the paint by ironing.

Painted fabric

 TIP

While you're painting, periodically lift up your fabric and move it to a clean, protected area before it dries. Moving the fabric will prevent it from sticking to the surface covering and will also keep any paint that puddles underneath from seeping up into the fabric in undesired areas.

Stamping

Supplies Needed:

- Prewashed fabric or pieced quilt top
- Commercial or handmade stamps
- Fabric or acrylic paints
- Small foam brushes, or brayer and printing plate or palette
- Iron

1. Apply pigment to a commercial or handmade stamp with a foam brush, dip the stamp into paint that has been spread onto a printing plate or palette, or roll paint onto the stamp with a brayer.

Apply paint to the stamp.

2. Stamp images onto the background fabric or quilt top.

Create a pattern or design with stamps.

3. Continue stamping until you have created an interesting composition with the stamped images. Wait for the paint to dry, and then layer more stamped images.

4. Heat set the paint by ironing.

Stamped fabric

2 Dragonflies, by Elin Waterston (quilt made with stamped and painted fabrics)

■ CLEANING UP

Fabric and acrylic paints are permanent! Brushes and stamps must be cleaned thoroughly using cold water and soap, before the pigment dries, or it will never come out.

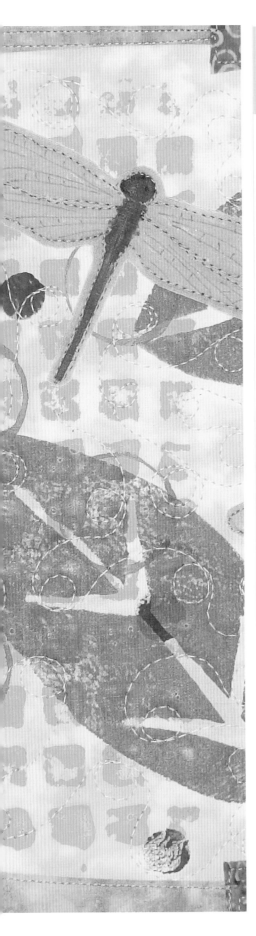

EXERCISE FOUR:
Foiling With Glue

Supplies Needed:

- Fabric or pieced quilt top
- Foiling glue
- Small brush or fine-tipped spouted bottle
- Foil sheets
- Burnishing tool (optional)
- Pressing cloth
- Iron

1. Paint a small shape or design onto a small piece of fabric or a quilt top with foiling glue, either with a small brush or a fine-tipped spouted bottle.

Apply glue to the fabric.

2. Allow the glue to dry completely—until it's clear.

3. Place the foil, color side up (shiny side, if you're using silver), so that it covers the glued area.

4. Press the back of the foil sheet with a burnishing tool, your finger, or your fingernail until the foil transfers to the glue, or cover the foil with a pressing cloth and iron to transfer the foil (and allow to cool).

Press the foil sheet onto the dry glue.

5. Carefully peel away the cellophane.

Peel away the cellophane.

Foil design on fabric

Foiling With Fusible Web

Supplies Needed:

- Fusible web
- Fabric or pieced quilt top
- Foil sheets
- Appliqué pressing sheet or parchment paper
- Pressing cloth
- Iron

1. Cut or tear the desired shape from fusible web.

Cut the shape from the fusible web.

2. Press the fusible shape onto the *right side* of a piece of fabric or a quilt top, web side down, using an appliqué pressing sheet or a piece of parchment paper.

3. Peel away the paper.

Peel away the paper.

4. Place the foil, color side up, onto the web, making sure it's covering the whole fusible shape.

Place the foil on the fabric.

5. Cover the foil with a pressing cloth and press for about 10 seconds with a medium-hot, dry iron.

6. Allow the foil to cool completely.

7. Carefully peel away the cellophane.

Peel away the cellophane.

Foil shape on fabric

 TIP

Save any cellophane sheets that have foil left on them—they can be reused until all the foil has been transferred.

"Creative people are curious, flexible, persistent, and independent, with a tremendous spirit of adventure and a love of play." —HENRI MATISSE

References for Further Exploration

WEBSITES OF QUILT ARTISTS

These quilt artists include painted or printed fabric in their work.

Bean Gilsdorf http://www.beangilsdorf.com/

Velda Newman http://www.veldanewman.com/

BOOKS

Beevers, Sue. *Off-the-Shelf Fabric Painting.* C&T Publishing: Lafayette, CA, 2004.

Dunnewold, Jane. *Complex Cloth: A Comprehensive Guide to Surface Design.* Martingale, 1996.

Kahn, Sherrill. *Creating With Paint: New Ways, New Materials.* Martingale: Bothell, WA, 2001.

Kahn, Sherrill. *Creative Stamping With Mixed Media Techniques.* North Light Books: Cincinnati, OH, 2003.

Noble, Elin. *Dyes and Paints: A Hands-On Guide to Coloring Fabric.* Fiber Studio Press: Bothell, WA, Martingale, 1998.

Udell, Luann. *Rubber Stamp Carving: Techniques, Designs & Projects.* Lark Books: New York, 2002.

Reflective Queries and Thinking Exercises

- Look at ordinary objects for their design.

- Stamp with leaves, fruits and vegetables, bubble wrap, and household and kitchen tools. (Remember that if you use a kitchen utensil for stamping, don't use it again for food).

- Get familiar with ways to use paintbrushes to achieve different looks.

- Try unique methods to get pigment onto fabric—like dripping or squirting it on with a ketchup bottle or a syringe, or spattering it on with a toothbrush.

Artists to Study

Pablo Picasso	André Derain
Odilon Redon	Jackson Pollock
Mark Rothko	Jean-Michel Basquiat
Paul Cezanne	Raoul Dufy
Gustav Klimt	Thomas Dewing
Florine Stettheimer	Friedensreich Hundertwasser

Chapter 6 Homework

Experiment with various stamping and painting techniques covered in this chapter.

Carve or make an original stamp.

Create a new (9″ × 12″, vertical) quilt using any or all these techniques.

THREAD WORK

This chapter's lesson covers various ways of using thread as a design element.

"A line is a dot that went for a walk." —PAUL KLEE

thread, *n.* A thin strand or filament of a natural or manufactured material, used in sewing or weaving (from Old English *threed,* related to *prawan:* to turn or twist).

Expressive Thread

Decorative threads

Thread painting, bobbin drawing, couching, and free-motion quilting are all means of visual expression that use thread as a medium. These techniques let you create an image completely out of thread, or enhance or emphasize an existing design. The effects that can be achieved with thread work are as numerous as the types of thread available.

Pears: Thread, by Elin Waterston

Dream, by Jane Dávila (quilt incorporating thread painting)

Bird in a Cage, by Elin Waterston (quilt with thread painting)

As in most artistic endeavors, experimentation and practice are the key to mastering thread-work skills. The more familiar you become with your tools and materials, the more comfort and confidence you will have. Decorative and novelty threads vary greatly—each requires different handling, as does each project's chosen fabric and batting. You must be willing to spend time testing and adjusting your machine's stitch tension and practicing your approach.

THREAD PAINTING

Using free-motion machine embroidery, you can create a "painting" of thread. By layering various threads, you can build an image on the fabric or quilt top, shading and filling in until the image is complete.

Thread painting can be done on collaged or appliquéd elements to add detail and texture to a design, or thread can be directly applied to a background to create an entire design with thread.

BOBBIN DRAWING

Bobbin drawing is done from the back of a piece, so the bobbin thread is what ultimately shows on the front. Usually, bobbin drawing uses threads that are too thick to go through a sewing machine's upper tension plates and the eye of the needle. The bobbin case can be adjusted to allow for the thickness of the threads. Using heavier thread creates a line that is cleaner and more well defined than the line you can get with a lighter-weight thread, resulting in a more dramatic effect. This method can be used on a quilt top as a surface-design element, or it can be used through the top, batting, and backing, as the quilting.

With this technique, you can stitch a design freehand or follow a design you draw on the back of the fabric, on the quilt backing, or on a piece of tracing paper (which you stitch through and then remove). Since the thread used for bobbin drawing is thick, the bobbin won't hold as much length as it would for regular-weight thread. It's a good idea to build starts and stops into your stitching design so you can refill the bobbin before you run out of thread.

Coqui, by Elin Waterston (quilt made with a representational bobbin drawing as part of the quilting design)

Lunar Enigma, by Jane Dávila

TIP

Since bobbin drawing involves adjusting the bobbin case tension, you might like to have an extra bobbin case explicitly for this purpose.

COUCHING

Some novelty yarns and threads are too thick or fuzzy to go through either the upper or lower tension mechanism. These fibers can be couched in place. Couching is the process of laying a thread, yarn, or fiber on the surface and stitching it in place, either by machine (with a straight or a zigzag stitch) or by hand. Couching results in a strong linear design and added surface texture.

You can couch threads by following a lightly drawn line (since the couched thread will cover the line) or by just laying down random designs. Machine couching tends to flatten decorative thread somewhat. Hand couching gives you a bit more control in maintaining the three-dimensionality of the decorative thread.

HAND STITCHING

Hand-quilting stitches can add texture and dimension to an art quilt, and need not be used strictly in the traditional manner. Hand stitching in contrasting thread can add a design element or emphasize existing designs.

Detail of *La Avispa* **(page 7)**

QUILTING DESIGNS

The quilting that holds your work together is an important part of the overall design—whether it's minimal straight lines or intricate free-motion patterns. Quilting can be merely a design that complements the elements of the work, or it can itself be representational. If you have a garden scene, you might choose to quilt it by outlining or echoing the design elements or by free-motion quilting flower or leaf shapes across the surface of the piece. Think of the quilting lines themselves as another element of your composition.

A good way to audition quilting designs is to draw potential designs on a clear overlay over a *drawing* of your quilt top (use a drawing of the quilt, rather than the actual quilt, to avoid inadvertently getting ink on the quilt top). Depending on the size of your piece, you can use overhead transparency sheets (the wipe-off type) or clear upholstery vinyl. Try out different quilting patterns by drawing them on the overlay with a wipe-off marker.

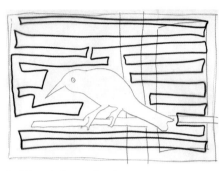

Quilting design option 1

Quilting design option 2

Tiger Fish, by Elin Waterston

Return 4, by Elin Waterston

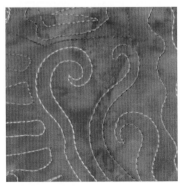

Detail of *Tiger Fish*

"Drawing is like making an expressive gesture with the advantage of permanence." –HENRI MATISSE

EXERCISE ONE: Thread Painting

Supplies Needed:

- Machine embroidery hoop
- Background fabric, at least 5″ larger than your hoop
- Drawing pencil
- Lightbox (optional)
- Rayon and cotton threads in a variety of colors
- 75/11 embroidery needle
- Free-motion/darning foot

1. With a pencil, draw a design onto the background fabric, making sure that the whole shape fits inside your machine embroidery hoop. You can draw the design first on paper and copy it onto your fabric, or draw it freehand directly on the fabric.

 TIP

When using a medium or dark background fabric, use a lightbox to trace your design onto the fabric.

2. Lay the outer hoop on a table; center the fabric, right side up, over the hoop so your design fits inside the hoop; and place the inner hoop inside the outer hoop.

Place the fabric on the outer hoop, right side up.

Place the inner hoop inside the outer hoop.

3. Tighten the outer hoop and pull the fabric as taut as you can while keeping the integrity of the grain.

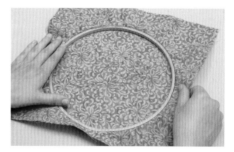

Tighten the outer hoop and pull the fabric taut.

4. Thread your sewing machine with a regular-weight cotton or rayon thread, with a matching thread in the bobbin, either regular weight or lighter embroidery weight.

5. Using a 75/11 embroidery needle and a free-motion/darning foot, and with the feed dogs dropped, free-motion draw the outline of your shape with a straight stitch.

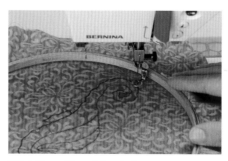

Stitch the outline of the design.

6. Fill in the shape by moving the hoop around under the needle, using a straight stitch or a zigzag stitch. Experiment with different stitch widths and different motions, and try shading and highlighting the shape with other colors of thread.

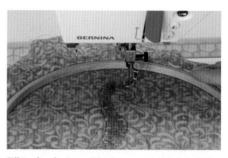

Fill in the design with zigzag or straight stitch.

Completed thread painting

 TIP

Once you've mastered this technique, you can move on to more complex thread-painting designs. If your design is larger than the usable area of your hoop, stitch the design elements within the hoop and then stop at a spot near the edge of the hoop (where the design will continue), sink the needle into the fabric, release the hoop and move it to another area of the fabric. Be sure to pull the fabric taut!

EXERCISE TWO:
Bobbin Drawing

Supplies Needed:

- Paper
- Pencil
- Heavy decorative thread (for example, Madeira Décor, YLI Pearl Crown rayon, perle cotton)
- Coordinating 40- or 50-weight cotton or rayon thread
- Fabric sandwich (the top of the sandwich can be either a pieced or fused quilt top or just a piece of fabric), 9˝ × 12˝
- 75/11 quilting needle
- Free-motion/darning foot (or walking foot for straight lines)
- Small screwdriver
- Small box or zip-close bag

1. On a piece of paper, draw a meandering pattern that you would like to replicate in thread.

2. Wind a bobbin with a heavy decorative thread.

3. Loosen the tension on the bobbin case to allow the decorative thread to slide through it by carefully turning the screw on the case (a little at a time) counterclockwise.

 TIP

Make a diagram of the starting position of the screw, so you can readjust it later.

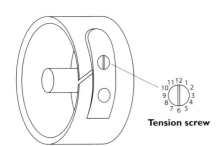

Adjust the bobbin tension.

Tension screw

 **TIP**

Adjust the bobbin tension while holding the bobbin case over a box or inside a zip-close bag, just in case the screw or the spring falls out while you're making the adjustment.

4. Test the bobbin tension with the "yo-yo" method: place the wound bobbin in the bobbin case and suspend the bobbin by holding the end of the thread in one hand with your other hand under the bobbin. Gently jerk the hand holding the thread. If the bobbin doesn't drop at all, the tension is too tight. If the bobbin drops into your hand, it's too loose. If the bobbin drops slightly and then stops, the tension is just right!

Test the bobbin tension.

5. Once the tension is correct, load the bobbin into the machine. Thread coordinating 40- or 50-weight, cotton or rayon thread through the top of the machine. Use a 75/11 quilting needle and a free-motion/darning foot.

TIP

Practice on a test sandwich. Once you've sewn a bit, check the front side of the sandwich to see whether the tension needs to be adjusted. If the top thread is showing on the front, either loosen the bobbin tension or tighten the top tension.

6. Lower the feed dogs and place your fabric sandwich, right side down, under the presser foot.

7. Lower the presser foot, hold onto the top thread, and sink and raise the needle once.

8. Pull the tail of the top thread to raise the bobbin thread up to the top of your work, which is actually the back of the fabric sandwich (stay with us—we know it's confusing).

9. Take a few small stitches to lock the threads.

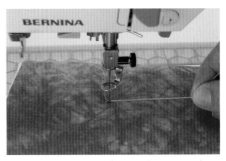

Pull up the bobbin thread and anchor the stitches.

10. Move the sandwich under the needle to create a design.

Move the sandwich under the needle to create the desired design.

11. When you've finished your design, take a few more small stitches to lock the thread, or pull the bobbin thread through to the top (you can knot it and thread it back into the sandwich with a hand-sewing needle to bury it).

◼ **TIP**

Remember that whatever you draw will be reversed on the front of the quilt—this is especially important when you're writing something!

Completed bobbin drawing

◼ **TIP**

When removing the bobbin from the bobbin case, cut the tail of the thread close to the case and then remove the bobbin, rather than dragging the tail back through the bobbin tension mechanism. This eliminates extra wear and tear on the bobbin case.

EXERCISE THREE:
Couching

Supplies Needed:

- Background fabric, 9″ × 12″
- Stabilizer
- Couching foot or open-toe embroidery foot
- Heavy decorative thread, yarn, or ribbon
- 40- or 50-weight thread (cotton or rayon)
- 75/11 embroidery needle or universal needle
- Small scissors

1. Place a piece of stabilizer underneath the 9″ × 12″ piece of background fabric.

2. If you have a couching foot, pass the decorative thread to be couched through the hole in the foot. If you don't have a couching foot, use an open-toe embroidery foot and lay the decorative thread down across the background fabric. Be sure to cut a generous length of decorative thread.

3. With a 40- or 50- weight thread (cotton or rayon) through a 75/11 embroidery needle or universal needle, anchor the decorative thread in place with a few small straight stitches.

Anchor the decorative thread.

4. Straight stitch or zigzag over the entire length of the decorative thread in your desired design.

Sew over the decorative thread.

5. When you have completed your design, take a few small straight stitches to anchor the end of the thread, and carefully trim off the excess close to the stitches, with small scissors.

6. Remove the stabilizer.

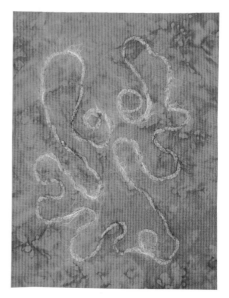

Completed couched design

◼ **TIP**

If you couch after the quilt has been layered and basted, use a walking foot and quilting needle.

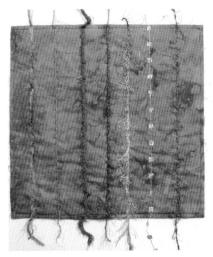

Various couched threads

References for Further Exploration

WEBSITES OF QUILT ARTISTS

These quilt artists use decorative thread techniques in their work.

Ellen Anne Eddy http://www.ellenanneeddy.com/

Christine Fries-Ureel http://www.loveabideth.com/

Libby Lehman http://www.libbylehman.us/

Nancy Prince http://www.nancyprince.com/

Melanie Testa http://www.melanietesta.com/

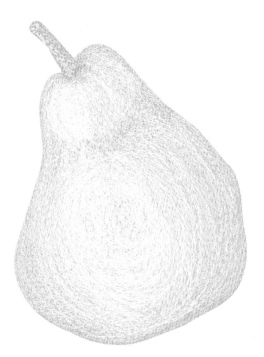

BOOKS

Eddy, Ellen Anne. *Thread Magic: The Enchanted World of Ellen Anne Eddy.* Quilting Arts: Stow, MA, 2005.

Noble, Maurine, and Elizabeth Hendricks. *Machine Quilting With Decorative Threads.* Martingale: Bothell, WA, 1998.

Prince, Nancy. *Quilt Savvy: Simple Thread Painting.* American Quilter's Society: Paducah, KY, 2004.

REFLECTIVE QUERIES AND THINKING EXERCISES

- Thread paint using different weights and types of threads (rayon, metallic, variegated color) to see what different effects can be achieved.

- Do continuous line contour drawings of some simple subjects and think about how you can translate them into thread or bobbin drawings.

- Couch the same decorative thread with various threads through the needle—metallic, rayon, and cotton threads, and contrasting and matching colors will give different looks to your finished project.

- Study a quilt top that hasn't been quilted yet and determine ways different quilting patterns would enhance the design.

- Look for lines! Look at things around you (like a bowl of fruit, a plant, or even a person or a pet) in terms of how they could be interpreted in thread.

Artists to Study

The work of these artists includes bold lines and contours.

Paul Klee   Lee Krasner   Alexander Calder

Keith Haring   Piet Mondrian

Chapter 7 Homework

Experiment with and practice the thread-work methods discussed in this chapter. Incorporate decorative thread work into one of your quilts from a previous chapter, or start a new piece expressly for thread work.

FOUND OBJECTS

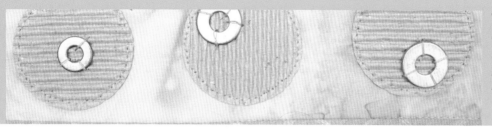

This chapter's lesson covers the use of found objects in art, methods of attaching found objects, and the archival considerations of using found objects.

"Passion is in all great searches and is necessary to all creative endeavors." —W. EUGENE SMITH

found object, *n.* A natural object or an artifact not originally intended as art, found and considered to have aesthetic value. Also called *objet trouvé.*

Perchance to Dream, **by Jane Dávila**

Finding Objects

Look around you! Objects that are not too heavy or too fragile, that are mostly two-dimensional, and that are not too big work best in art quilts. You are limited only by your imagination.

Paper Dolls, by Elin Waterston (quilt with small scissors attached by hand)

Archival Considerations

Fabric, although long lasting, has a limited life span. Some objects in contact with fabric will cause it to deteriorate. Anything acidic (some inks, some glues, and some natural or man-made found objects) will cause deterioration. Anything that you wouldn't expect to last if left alone for a week or two is probably not a good choice for a found object.

Many natural objects will work well if first coated with a water-based polyurethane or gel medium. Most art papers are acid-free and thus safe to use. Coated metal is fine, plastic is fine, objects made of fabric are fine. Some found objects that will cause harm to the quilt (rusting metal, for example) can be added to quilts intentionally. It is important to be aware of the choices you are making. When in doubt, experiment and do some research.

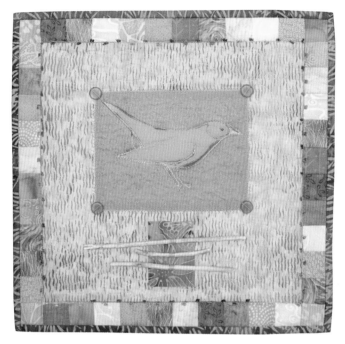

Sweet Harmony, by Elin Waterston (quilt with twigs sewn on using embroidery floss)

Found Objects

PAPER

A variety of paper—mulberry, card stock, cardboard, handmade, printed, vellum

Paper is a versatile found object! Art papers and watercolor papers are ideal for incorporation into art quilts. You can draw, sketch, or paint on paper; fold, cut, tear, or emboss it; sew it on; glue it on; or attach it with other found objects. Handmade papers made from cotton, mulberry, or other plant material are especially beautiful. Consider also postage stamps, parts of greeting cards, tags, and seed packs. Corrugated cardboard pulled apart makes an interesting texture. Card stock and mat board can work well.

WIRE

A variety of wire—copper, aluminum, covered, colored

You can use copper, aluminum, silver, colored, and telephone wire, as well as paper clips and staples. Make sure the wire is coated or sealed or it will oxidize and rust.

NATURAL OBJECTS

A variety of natural objects

Consider using leaves, dried flowers, dried fruit, seeds, pods, feathers, shells, rocks, and so on. Anything that is juicy or decomposing is not a good choice. Coat or seal it, if possible, if you're in doubt.

MAN-MADE OBJECTS

A variety of man-made objects

Look around—inspiration is everywhere! Pop tops, twist ties, washers, nuts, rubber bands, keys, watch gears, circuit boards, and so on. Anything that is dirty or greasy or that has exposed, uncoated metal might not be a good choice.

Tools

An assortment of tools

Some handy tools to have around when working with found objects include pliers, a small hammer, wire cutters, scissors of every type, tin snips, round-tipped jewelry pliers, a brad setter, an electric drill, a small hand saw, an awl, a hole punch, and a wood presser.

Attaching Found Objects

You can attach found objects before or after quilting, and before or after you attach another element to your quilt.

SEWING BY HAND

If the object can be sewn through easily, you can use either thread or wire to attach it. If the object is somewhat difficult to get a needle through, sew along the sides you'd like to stitch down using your sewing machine and a large needle (with no thread) to make perforations. You will be able to use these perforated holes for hand stitching. Another option is to punch holes in the object with an awl or to drill small holes through it. If you can't make a hole in the object, consider holding it down by sewing over it. You may need to use a drop of glue to hold it in place while you sew, if you can't pin it.

Halcyon Summer, by Jane Dávila (quilt incorporating mulberry paper, paper mesh, and sea glass attached by hand)

SEWING BY MACHINE

You need an appropriate needle: a small needle for delicate, thin, fragile objects and a heavier needle for thicker, tougher, sturdier objects. Consider using a blanket stitch, feather stitch, or zigzag stitch. Consider multiple rows of stitching, all in one color or in different colors.

Re-Grouping, by Jane Dávila (quilt incorporating mulberry paper and basket caning attached by machine)

GLUE OR ACRYLIC GEL MEDIUM

Glue works well on flatter objects, on objects with no protrusions that might catch on something, on porous objects, and on light objects. An alternative to glue is acrylic gel medium. It can be used both as an adhesive and as a surface sealant. Gel medium is available in a variety of finishes and even in different textures. Your choice of finish will let you change the surface quality of an object—you can change something from glossy to matte and vice versa.

WIRE

Wire itself is a found object, but it can also be used to attach other found objects to your quilt. It can be used as a hand-sewing "thread" if it is thin and flexible enough. If it is a little thicker and less flexible, you may need to pre-punch holes in your quilt with a tailor's awl and use jewelry pliers to bend the wire into position. The ends can be bent over on the back and stitched in place with thread. Wire can also be couched down by hand or machine as a surface element.

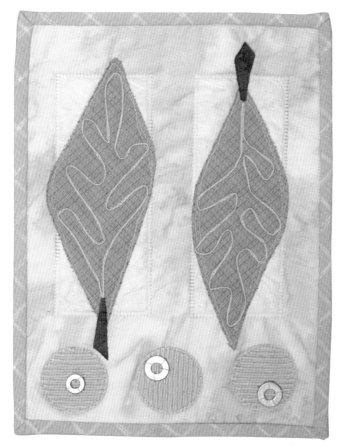

Maine Reflections: Leaf Textures, by Jane Dávila (quilt incorporating mulberry paper, corrugated cardboard, brass washers, and paper raffia, using glue to aid positioning)

Maine Reflections: Schooner, by Jane Dávila (quilt incorporating handmade paper, metal brads, and copper wire couched by machine)

FUSIBLES

Some flat, lightweight found objects can be backed with fusible web before being sewn to a background. This step can add stability to a delicate object and help protect the edges. However, you should experiment first to make sure the heat from the iron or the glue in the fusible won't damage the object.

Llaves, by Jane Dávila (quilt with fused textured paper and printed paper elements)

EXERCISES

EXERCISE ONE: Working with Paper

Supplies Needed:

- Background fabric or a fabric sandwich, 8˝ × 8˝
- Assortment of paper
- Assortment of thread
- Glue
- Fusible web

1. Using paper and fabric, create a composition of simple shapes; the paper can be the main focus or can be added to a fabric composition.

2. Experiment with hand and machine stitching, gluing and fusing, and various weights and types of paper.

Clockwise from upper left: printed handmade paper sewn by hand with three strands of embroidery floss; mulberry paper sewn by machine with a blanket stitch; scrapbook papers glued on; and card stock sewn by machine with multiple rows of straight stitching

---

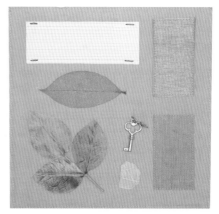

Clockwise from upper left: corrugated cardboard attached by hand with embroidery floss; copper mesh attached by machine with cotton thread; paper screening attached by machine with cotton thread; sea glass attached by hand with linen thread; antique artificial leaves attached with fusible web; skeleton leaf attached with gel medium; and center, key charm attached with 20-gauge copper wire

"Art is long, life short, judgment difficult, opportunity transient. To act is easy, to think is hard; to act according to our thought is troublesome. Every beginning is cheerful; the threshold is the place of expectation."

—JOHANN WOLFGANG VON GOETHE

References for Further Exploration

WEBSITES OF ARTISTS
These collage/mixed-media fiber artists use found objects in their work.

Dale Copeland http://virtual.tart.co.nz/Dale/dale.htm

Janet Ghio http://www.quiltcollage.com/

Jerry Jackson http://www.jerryjackson.com/

Linda Leonhard http://www.lindaleonhard.com/

Janice Lowry http://www.janicelowry.com/

Lesley Riley http://www.lalasland.com/

BOOKS
Hellmuth, Claudine. *Collage Discovery Workshop*. North Light Books: Cincinnati, OH, 2003.

Michel, Karen. *The Complete Guide to Altered Imagery*. Quarry Books: Gloucester, MA, 2005.

Riley, Leslie. *Quilted Memories: Journaling, Scrapbooking & Creating Keepsakes With Fabric*. Sterling Publications: New York, 2005.

Smiley, Jane Bode. *The Art of Fabric Books: Innovative Ways to Use Fabric in Scrapbooks, Altered Books & More*. C&T Publishing: Lafayette, CA, 2005.

Waldman, Diane. *Collage, Assemblage, and the Found Object*. H.N. Abrams: New York, 1992.

Reflective Queries and Thinking Exercises

- What makes a good found object for an art quilt?

- Look at the shapes and colors of everyday objects. Play with a box of paper clips or elbow macaroni.

- Find an object that is unrecognizable out of context. Choose an object for its surface qualities, color, or shape.

Artists to Study

These artists use found objects or mixed-media techniques in their work.

Betye Saar	Kurt Schwitters	Marcel Duchamp	Jasper Johns
Joseph Cornell	Louise Nevelson	Robert Rauschenberg	

Chapter 8 Homework

Incorporate one or more found objects into one of your (9″ × 12″, vertical) quilts, or start a new quilt for found objects.

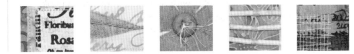

EMBELLISHING

This chapter covers an array of embellishments and various methods of attaching them.

"An artist must educate himself; he cannot be educated. He must test things out as they apply to himself; his life is one long investigation of things and his own reaction to them. If he is to be interesting to us it is because he renders a very personal account." —ROBERT HENRI

embellish, v. 1. To make beautiful with ornamentation, decorate. 2. To heighten the attractiveness of by adding ornamental details, enhance (from Latin *bellus*: beautiful).

When to Embellish

Embellishments can help create a mood or help define a focal point; they can add individuality to your quilt. The choice to use embellishments, either sparingly or heavily, is personal. Think about the attributes of your embellishments, including their surface (shiny or matte), their size (large or small), and their variety (differences or sameness). The goal is to enhance your quilt, not to overpower it. You may choose to cover your quilt with 10,000 seed beads as a design choice, causing the beads to become the composition, or you may use one shisha mirror to emphasize your focal point.

Amor Eterno, by Elin Waterston

Shrine I, by Jane Dávila

Shrine II, by Jane Dávila

The decision about whether to embellish before or after layering and quilting is also personal. Items added before layering will sit on the surface of the quilt, whereas items added after layering will sink into the surface. You must also consider the appearance of the back of the quilt.

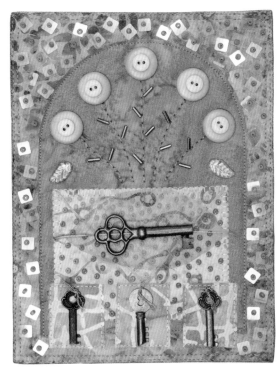

Shrine III, by Jane Dávila

Shrine IV, by Jane Dávila

 TIP

There are several options for dealing with the back of your embellished quilt. If you attach embellishments after layering and quilting, you can hide all your knots between the backing and batting. You could add another false back over a previous back and add a few lines of quilting to secure the layers. You could decide that you don't care what the back looks like and let it all hang out. This is art after all—people rarely if ever look at the back of an oil painting. There are other methods and combinations of these methods to use for your quilt back. Choose what works best for your piece, its intended audience, and your comfort level.

Embellishments

A variety of embellishments

BEADS

Beads are available in a vast variety of materials and shapes. There are small round beads, often made of glass, referred to as seed beads; bugles (tube-shaped glass beads); cut-glass and crystal beads; pearls and semi-precious beads; metal beads; plastic beads; ceramic and porcelain beads; and wooden beads. You can also make beads from, among other things, paper, fabric, wax, wire, and polymer clay.

Beads can be sewn on singly, doubly, or continuously; couched; used as fringe in stalks; edgestitched; or used as fill or in combination with other embellishments and embroidery. Some beads can be sewn by machine, but the majority will be sewn by hand, using the basic backstitch. A stronger thread than usual is used. Beads can also be used to secure sequins and buttons.

Couch beads by stringing them onto a length of beading thread inserted into a fabric and sewing over this thread with another thread. Take a stitch between each bead to hold it in place, forming a pattern or following a line.

Couching beads by hand

Detail of *Shrine II* (page 71), showing beads couched in a curved line

Scatter stitch beads randomly, sparsely, or densely, using a back-stitch. The effect is that of beads tossed onto a quilt.

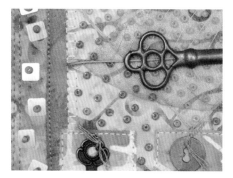

Detail of *Shrine III* (page 71), showing scatter-stitched beads

Make a bead fringe by starting with a stitch at the bottom of a quilt or element. String a row of beads and go back through all but the bottom bead and end where you started. Knot the ends of the thread on the back.

Detail of *Shrine I* (page 70), showing a bead fringe, with beads of various sizes

Edgestitch beads by starting with a stitch at the bottom of a quilt or element. String an odd number of beads and re-enter the fabric at a distance that is shorter than the length of the strung beads. Repeat to form a scalloped edge of beads.

Detail of *Shrine I* (page 70), showing edgestitched beads that form a scallop

BUTTONS

Buttons come in sizes from tiny to well over two inches across, and in every shape imaginable, including representational and geometric. They are fashioned from a vast array of materials, both natural and man-made. They may be sew-through buttons (with two or four holes), or they may have self-shanks or attached shanks.

Sew-through buttons can be sewn on with the thread ends on the back or tied on the front leaving the ends of the thread as part of the embellishment.

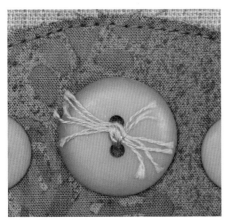

Detail of *Shrine IV* (page 71), showing button attached with embroidery floss

Buttons of various sizes can be stacked and sewn on through their holes.

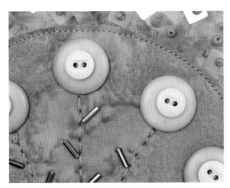

Detail of *Shrine III* (page 71), showing stacked buttons

Buttons can be set closely together, with edges overlapping, randomly or in a pattern.

Detail of *Toward Femininity* (page 26), showing buttons set together, forming a pattern

Buttons can be sewn on by machine or by hand with matching or contrasting thread in a variety of weights. Try sewing a button on from the outside in over the edges.

Detail of *Shrine IV* (page 71), showing button sewn from the outside in, with the stitching forming a pattern

Buttons with large shanks can be placed in holes punched through the quilt with an awl. Buttons with small shanks can be sewn on tightly to sink into the surface of the quilt. Beads can be used on top of buttons.

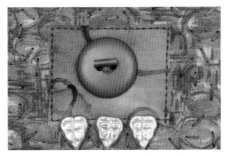

Detail of *Shrine II* (page 71), showing button sewn with a bead

SHISHA MIRRORS

Shisha mirrors appear traditionally in Russian and Central Asian (especially Indian and Pakistani) embroidery. They are pieces of mica or mirror glass applied to fabric. Shisha come in a variety of sizes and shapes, including round, oblong, triangular, and square. The color can vary from silver to gold, green, or blue. No holes are drilled in shisha, and they are held in place by a network of thread. The middle part is exposed, and the edges are covered with stitches.

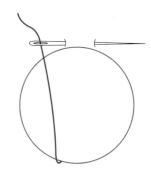

Detail of *Shrine IV* (page 71), showing shisha hand sewn with embroidery floss

1. Holding the shisha firmly in place with your thumb, sew 2 parallel vertical stitches.

Sew very close to the edge of the mirror.

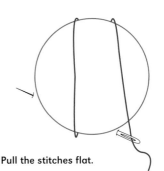

Pull the stitches flat.

2. Sew 2 horizontal stitches, looping under the first vertical stitches. Pull these 4 stitches fairly tight because all the following stitches will be attached to these.

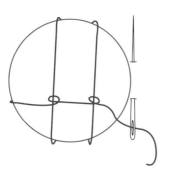

Loop under the first stitches.

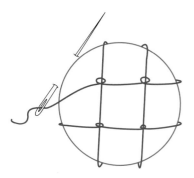

This grid forms the framework for the remaining stitches.

3. Slide the needle under the top left-hand intersection of stitches. Note: Contrasting thread is used for clarity.

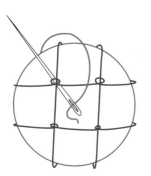

4. Enter the background and make a small chain stitch to the right at the outer edge of the shisha.

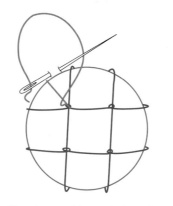

5. Continue taking stitches through the initial grid and forming chain stitches along the outer edge of the shisha until you have gone completely around the mirror.

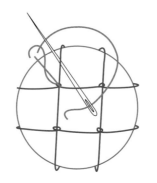

Remember to head in the same direction consistently.

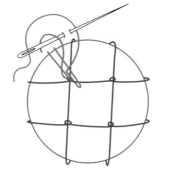

If desired, sew a second row of chain stitches around the finished shisha. Consider adding beads between and among these stitches.

SEQUINS

Also known as paillettes and spangles, sequins are shiny, thin metal or plastic shapes. Sequins are often flat but are sometimes indented into a cup shape. They are available in myriad colors and prints. When they match the fabric they're sewn onto, they add shimmer and texture.

Sequins can be attached by sewing from the back through the center, then through a bead, and then down through the center again.

Detail of *Shrine III* (page 71), showing sequins attached with beads

Sequins can also be sewn on singly, in rows, overlapping in rows, with decorative stitching, or upside down, with matching or contrasting thread.

Square sequins sewn in a row

Sequins can be sewn on with two, three, four, or more stitches over the edges.

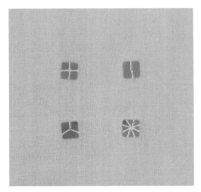

Sequins sewn on with a pattern of stitches

TRIMS

Many fabulous trims are available for embellishing your quilts, including beaded trim, rickrack, and ribbon in a vast variety of colors, sizes, and materials. Trims can be sewn to the surface of the quilt by hand or machine. They can be sewn to, or into, one or more edges of the quilt. They can be sewn into the piecing of the quilt. Ribbon can be topstitched, embroidered, couched, left partially loose, or tied through the quilt layers.

Trim can be attached to elements within a composition by topstitching, couching, layering, or even piecing. The scale of the trim should relate to the elements you add it to.

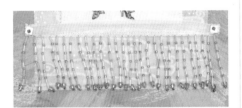

Detail of *Fashionable Women* (page 93), showing trim within a composition

Trim can also be added to the bottom edge of your quilt. You can catch the upper edge of the trim between the front and back layers or simply topstitch it to the front or to the back of the quilt.

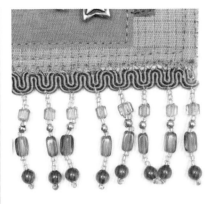

Detail of *Shrine IV* (page 71), showing trim attached to the bottom of a quilt

CHARMS AND MILAGROS

Charms are small metal shapes with a hole for attaching. They are either one sided or two sided and are usually figurative. Milagros (translation: miracles) are small charms from Mexico, which the faithful believe are endowed with spiritual or magical powers. Milagros can represent specific objects, people, animals, or symbolic concepts. Charms and milagros can be sewn on with a decorative thread, leaving the tails long.

La Virgen 2, by Elin Waterston

As with many small objects or elements, charms appear a more integral part of a composition if they are grouped together or used in combination with larger elements. If you cluster them or give them a defined space, they will have more impact than if you use them randomly.

Detail of *Shrine III* (page 71), showing charms grouped within other design elements

They can dangle from the bottom of the quilt or from an element on the quilt.

Detail of *Amor Eterno* (page 70), showing milagros dangling from a design element

They can be attached to the bottom of a bead fringe.

A bead fringe ending with a charm

EXERCISE ONE:
Combining Embellishments

Supplies Needed:

- Background fabric or a fabric sandwich, 6″ × 6″

- Assorted beads, sequins, buttons, shisha mirrors, charms

- Beading needles and beading threads

- Hand-sewing needles

- Various threads

1. Combine several embellishments —for example, beads and buttons; beads and sequins; shisha and beads; charms and buttons; and so on.

2. Experiment with various ways of attaching these embellishments to the background fabric or fabric sandwich.

EXERCISE TWO:
Edge Embellishments

Supplies Needed:

- Background fabric or a fabric sandwich, 6″ × 6″

- Assorted beads and charms

- Beading needles and beading threads

- Hand-sewing needles

- Various threads

1. Try creating a bead fringe both with and without a charm as the bottom embellishment on your background fabric or fabric sandwich.

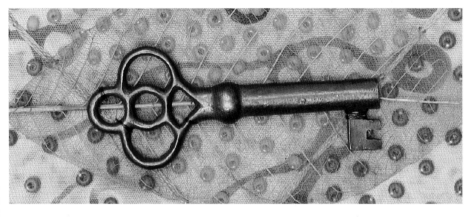

2. Edgestitch some beads, alternating the numbers of beads used in each scallop to study the effect.

References for Further Exploration

WEBSITES OF QUILT ARTISTS

These quilt artists use embellishments in their work.

Deana Hartman http://www.chameleonquilts.com/

Therese May http://theresemay.com/

Susan "Lucky" Shie http://www.turtlemoon.com/

Andrea Stern http://www.embellishmentcafe.com/

BOOKS

Brown, Pauline. *Decoration on Fabric*. Guild of Master Craftsmen: East Sussex, United Kingdom, 2001.

Campbell-Harding, Valerie, and Pamela Watts. *Bead Embroidery*. Batsford: London, United Kingdom, 1993.

Stori, Mary. *All-in-One Beading Buddy*. C&T Publishing: Lafayette, CA, 2005.

Stori, Mary. *Beading Basics*. C&T Publishing: Lafayette, CA, 2004.

Reflective Queries and Thinking Exercises

- Study an embellished quilt and consider how the embellishing impacts your reaction to it. Look at a quilt with no embellishing and consider how various embellishments might enhance it.

- When is embellishing too much?

Chapter 9 Homework

Continue working on all the quilts in your series, adding embellishments where desired, or start another quilt to highlight embellishment techniques. You should be nearly finished with the majority of your quilts.

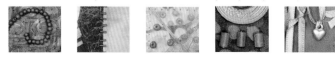

FINISHING TECHNIQUES

This chapter's lesson covers finishing and binding techniques and display methods.

"Have no fear of perfection; you'll never reach it." –SALVADOR DALI

artist, *n.* A person who practices or performs a creative art (from Latin *ars*: art).

Mind & Memory (Subway Station), **by Elin Waterston**

To Bind or Not to Bind

If you choose to use traditional binding, you can opt to vary the width of the cut strips to suit your taste and the scale of the work. For example, typical double-fold French binding strips are cut 2½″ wide. Try cutting the strips to 1¾″ for a narrower binding. See *Blue Zuzu* (page 92) for an example of a quilt with skinny binding.

Although binding is the traditional method of finishing a quilt, there are many alternative edge treatments that can be used. Decorative thread, cord, ribbon, or yarn can be couched over the edge. One side—or more—can be edged with rickrack, fringe, or piping. Edges can be finished with a straight stitch, satin stitch, or zigzag stitch around the perimeter of the piece, or the edges can be trimmed with pinking shears. Edges can be left raw or painted with fabric or acrylic paint.

If you prefer a no-binding look, the quilt can be enveloped or finished with the no-binding binding (page 80).

Detail of *Anticipation* (page 8), showing rickrack on bottom edge of quilt

Detail of *Halcyon Summer* (page 66), showing quilt edge painted with Jacquard Lumiere metallic paint

Detail of *Toward Femininity* (page 26), showing envelope finish

Labels

An assortment of labels

It is important to label your work with your name and address (or contact information, that is, phone number, email address, and so on), the size of the piece, the date of completion,

the copyright symbol, and the title of the piece. This information can be hand-written, typed and printed onto fabric, or embroidered by hand or machine. The title of the piece can be simple (*Untitled #1*) or descriptive (*Green Squares*), or it can be something that has emotional or personal meaning. The label can be basted in place before the piece is quilted, so it is held in place by the quilting stitches. It can also be attached after the piece is completed.

Hanging

Laughing Buddha, by Elin Waterston (quilt with a decorative hanging device)

Once you've finished a piece, you have several hanging options. The most common method is to attach a sleeve to the back of the quilt and insert a rod or slat for attaching the quilt to the wall. Sew fabric loops to secure a decorative pole to the top of the piece, so the hanging apparatus becomes part of the design. A quilt can be placed in a traditional frame, either with no glass or with glass and a spacer between the glass and the quilt. (Moisture can collect on the interior side of the glass—the spacer prevents the glass from touching the surface of the quilt and lets moisture evaporate without any damage to the artwork.)

Our Lady, by Elin Waterston (quilt matted and framed without glass)

Another option is to mount the quilt on canvas stretchers. To do this, center the quilt on a piece of fabric 8″–10″ larger than the quilt, facing up, and sew around the perimeter. Wrap the fabric around stretchers the size of the finished quilt, and staple the fabric securely in place on the back. Canvas stretchers are available in many standard lengths at art supply stores, or can be custom ordered to fit the quilt.

Red Cat (quilt mounted on canvas stretchers—front view)

Red Cat (quilt mounted on canvas stretchers—back view)

You can also mount the quilt on a prestretched, painted canvas. Purchase a primed cotton or linen stretched canvas with finished edges at least 2″ larger than your piece in all directions. The canvas is available in various depths from ¾″ to 2½″ deep and many widths. The area of excess canvas forms another border around the work and allows you an opportunity to add to your composition.

Paint the canvas (including the sides) with acrylic paint in a solid color or a pattern. Consider adding other elements (thread, found objects, embellishments) to the canvas as well. Attach your quilt to the canvas with hook-and-loop tape in several places, or discreetly sew the quilt directly to the canvas by hand (it is fabric after all!).

Encantada, by Jane Dávila (quilt mounted on a painted canvas)

 TIP

Some quilt shows require certain hanging methods or specific sleeve widths. Take these requirements into consideration when preparing a quilt for display.

Finishing Techniques

NO-BINDING BINDING

1. Cut 2 strips of fabric 1½˝ by the length of 2 opposite sides of the quilt.

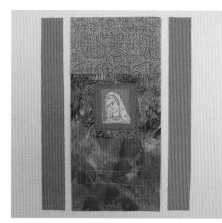

Cut strips.

2. Sew a strip to the front of each side of the quilt, with right sides together.

Attach strips.

3. Press the seam allowances toward the binding strips.

4. Turn the long raw edges of the strips under ¼˝ and press.

Press seam allowance and turn under edge.

5. Staystitch about ⅛˝ along the binding strip sides, with matching thread. (Note: Contrasting thread is used in the photo for visibility.)

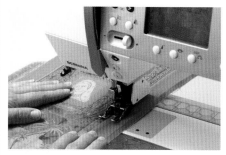

Staystitch binding.

6. Turn the strips under the quilt so they are not visible from the quilt's front side.

7. Hand stitch the strips in place on the back of the quilt.

Hand stitch in place.

8. Cut 2 strips 1½˝ by the length of the remaining 2 sides, plus 1˝.

9. Sew these strips to the quilt, leaving about ½˝ of extra fabric extending past each end. Press the seam allowances and staystitch along the edges.

Sew binding, leaving ½˝ on each side.

10. Turn the strips under the quilt, tucking in the extra ½˝ of fabric to create a finished edge at each end, and hand sew the binding in place on the back of the quilt.

Turn in raw edge.

Tuck under excess fabric.

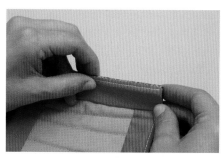

Turn strip under and hand sew in place.

Blue Madonna, by Elin Waterston (quilt finished with no-binding binding)

Reflective Queries and Thinking Exercises

- Experiment with various edge treatments.

- Try alternative hanging methods.

- How does the edge treatment or method of hanging affect the visual impact of a quilt?

Chapter 10 Homework

Finish the pieces you started for this series.

THE BUSINESS OF BEING AN ARTIST

This chapter's lesson covers information on exhibiting your work, marketing, and networking.

"The creative act is not performed by the artist alone; the spectator brings the work in contact with the external world by deciphering and interpreting its inner qualifications and thus adds his contribution to the creative act." —MARCEL DUCHAMP

exhibit, *v.* To display or present for others to see (from Latin *exhibere*: to hold).

Art & Nature, by Elin Waterston

How to Be Seen

EXHIBITING

To get your work seen, you have to put it out there! That means you have to enter as many exhibits as you can. You can enter local, national, or international quilt shows or look into general calls for entry at art galleries and museums. If you choose to enter an art show, make sure the organizers allow fiber art. Some exhibits specify "no crafts," which often includes art quilts. If you're uncertain about this, call or email and ask whether the show allows fiber art.

When you find a show that you wish to enter, the first step is to get the prospectus. A prospectus is a document with all the specifics and rules for entering a show, as well as the entry form. Each show's prospectus will vary but generally will include a calendar of important dates (entry deadlines, due dates, and dates of the exhibit), eligibility requirements, information about the juror or jurying procedure, applicable fees, and other entry requirements.

It is vital that you read and follow all the instructions exactly as they are outlined in the exhibit's prospectus. If the prospectus asks for one slide per piece, send only one! If the show has size requirements, stay within them.

Remember, there are usually ten times as many applicants (or more) as slots to fill, and the organizers will reject anyone who complicates the jurying process by not following the rules. And on that subject—be prepared for rejection. Nobody gets into every show every time!

Keep track of what pieces are entered where and when, and how long the commitment is. Don't double-book anything—wait until you get notification before entering a piece in the next show.

■ **TIP**

Once you've filled out an entry form, make a copy of the form and write the date that you entered on the copy. This record-keeping will help you keep track of what exhibits you've entered and what pieces were entered.

Most shows and galleries require slides for jurying. The quality of your artwork is only as good as the quality of your photography! Lots of good artists get rejected because of poor-quality slides. It is imperative that you have professional-quality slides. If you hire a professional photographer, find one with experience shooting art and fine crafts. You can also approach a college photography department and hire a student photographer. Either way, be sure to ask to see examples of the photographer's work and agree on a price before scheduling a shoot.

If you decide to shoot the slides your-self, set your work against a plain background with nothing else in the frame—like hands or feet! Frame the shot so the work fills the space with very little blank space around it. Be sure the work is well lit and in focus. Label all slides as required and mail them in a slide sleeve.

Sometimes a portfolio or presentation book will be required, so it's a good idea to have one and keep it up to date. Increasingly, galleries are accepting digital images for jurying. Again, good-quality images are crucial. Follow the size and labeling instructions outlined in the prospectus.

Presentation materials

Occasionally you'll be asked to send or hand deliver the actual piece for jurying. When doing this, make sure the piece is clean—no wrinkles or pet hair—and ready to hang, according to the show's requirements.

ARTIST'S STATEMENTS

For many exhibits, you will be asked to write an artist's statement. Sometimes the statement is specific to the work in the exhibit, and sometimes it's an overall statement of your body of work, style, and influences and the techniques you employ. Writing an artist's statement can be intimidating since it is usually quite personal. Keep your statement short and clear and make sure you fulfill any requirements that are requested for specific shows. Remember, however, that your work must speak for itself and not rely on a statement or explanation.

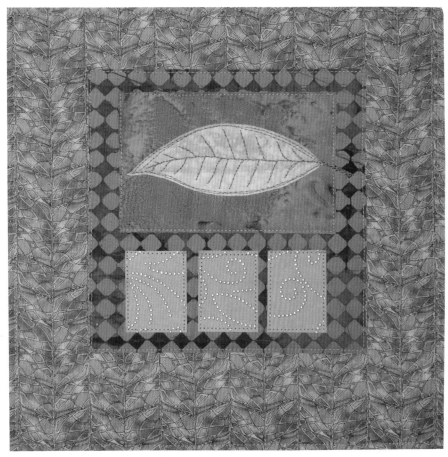

New Leaf, by Jane Dávila

PRICING YOUR WORK

Occasionally, a gallery will accept pieces that are not for sale (NFS) or price on request (POR), but most of the time galleries require a retail price at the time of entry. When pricing, keep in mind that some galleries retain up to 50 percent of the sale price. Before you get mad about this, remember that they have a lot of overhead—rent, utilities, advertising, and high, high, high insurance costs. Some artists use a price-per-square-foot (or square-inch) rule, and some calculate time and materials costs and price accordingly.

However you choose to price your work, keep a price list and be consistent—the price of any given piece should be the same if it is purchased through a gallery or directly from the artist. Ultimately, what's most important when pricing your work is that you get what you feel you need for each piece, to make it worth your time and effort.

DELIVERY AND SHIPPING

When you've been accepted into a show, you'll receive specific shipping instructions and deadlines. If your piece is too large to be shipped flat, it can be rolled on a Styrofoam "noodle," and shipped in a mailing tube or long box. Whether you ship your work flat or rolled, place it in a clear plastic bag to protect it from potential water damage, with all contact information on the inside as well as the outside of the box.

Most artists ship their work with a commercial shipping company, like UPS or FedEx, because they provide good tracking services. Be sure to include shipping insurance if your work is not covered by the gallery's insurance or your personal insurance. Most exhibitions require you to pay

return shipping as well, so include either a prepaid return shipping label or a check and detailed instructions for the return of the work. If the same box will be used for return shipping, write your name, the title of the piece, and instructions for return on the inside of the box.

Quilt rolled on a "noodle"

◼ TIP

Sometimes galleries request additional slides or photos of an accepted piece. Be prepared for this by keeping copies of slides of each piece on hand. The best way to keep slides organized is to place them in labeled slide sleeves when you have them processed. Keep them in a three-ring binder in alphabetical order, so it will be easy to find what you need when you need it. Keep one full shot and one detail of each work in a separate binder, so you'll have an original from which you can have duplicates made if needed. You might also be asked to send a resume and biography or slides or photos of other works. Keep your resume up to date and keep a file of extra photos, just in case.

INSURANCE

Many shows or galleries will insure work only while it's in their possession, and some don't offer any insurance. You can purchase a rider for your homeowner's policy that will cover all your art, at home and away. Most insurance companies require appraisals for quilts to be insured.

MARKETING

There are as many marketing strategies as there are types of artists! You'll need to find what works for you, but here are some general suggestions.

A website is an excellent publicity tool. Before you say "too hard" or "too expensive," consider some of the free or nearly free hosts with site-building software. Check with your Internet service provider's member services to see if they offer free space for personal web pages.

Business cards and contact cards are also great marketing tools. You can have cards printed professionally or print them yourself on your home computer. There are several brands of paper made specifically for business cards, or you can use the larger, post-card-size contact cards. Be sure to include all the contact information needed (name, address, phone number, email address), a photo of one of your pieces, and your web address.

Business and contact cards

Another way of making your art visible is art gallery representation. Before approaching a gallery, do some research. Visit many galleries to find one that will be a good fit for your work. Ask in person or by phone whether the gallery you've chosen is currently reviewing slides. When sending a package for review, choose ten to twenty slides (the number depends on how many the gallery requests) of current work. Make sure your slides are labeled with your name and the titles, dimensions, media, and years of execution of the works.

Your package should also include a cover letter stating that you would like this gallery to represent you; a self-addressed, stamped envelope for the return of your materials; a current biography; a brief statement about your work; and a retail price list. You can also include a short description of your process.

Galleries receive many, many applications for review and may take three months or longer to respond. Again, don't be put off by rejection. Send the returned slides right out to the next gallery on your list.

CONTRACT

Once you've been accepted by a gallery for representation, you will be asked to sign a contract. This contract will cover such things as exclusivity, pricing, percentages, payment, and exhibiting in their venue and in other venues. You may want to discuss the terms of the contract with a lawyer before signing.

Galleries can reach museums, collectors, corporations, and others that you couldn't access on your own, and can help you gain recognition, increase your prices, and expand your market. Having a gallery represent you also allows you to concentrate on your work while someone else handles the business end.

There are, however, a few disadvantages to gallery representation. A percentage of your retail selling price—typically 40–60 percent—will go to the gallery. This percentage can include all sales, whether they are made through the gallery or not. There may be restrictions on where you can exhibit and how you price your work. You need to weigh the pros and cons and decide whether the deal is right for you.

If you're not sure whether gallery representation is right for you, consider joining a co-op gallery. Usually a co-op gallery requires that you pay a yearly membership fee in exchange for the opportunity to exhibit year-round in member shows. You might also be required to put in a certain number of hours of gallery sitting or office work as part of your membership.

Find out who the arts editors are for your local papers. Keep them informed via press releases of all your artistic news, including studio tours, exhibits, and prizes.

COMMISSIONS

When you have an opportunity for commission work, either through personal or gallery connections or from website visitors, it's important to have all the expectations (for both parties—artist and purchaser) laid out in a commission agreement or contract. Among other things, this contract should include price (including applicable taxes), all pertinent dates or deadlines, copyright and ownership information, resale rights, and a clear plan for what happens if either party should default. Make sure to include a payment schedule. Usually, the price is paid in two or three equal installments with a portion paid to the artist when contracts are signed, and the final portion on delivery of the finished work.

Return 2, **by Elin Waterston**

NETWORKING

Although most art is created alone, getting together with like-minded people has its advantages. Networking, either in person or via the Internet, can lead to unexpected opportunities and can further your professional development. Most large towns and cities have an artists' guild. These guilds often offer classes, sponsor exhibitions, and host lectures.

Art quilting and surface design both have several professional organizations you can join. Most of these have no meetings (although several sponsor yearly conferences), but they do have newsletters and other publications, Internet groups, and local representation. These organizations are invaluable resources for the professional and business side of the art. There are also often exhibition and sales opportunities available.

Consider starting or joining a small group of artists—either all working in fiber, or working in different media—for support and critique.

"Art is an experience, not an object." –ROBERT MOTHERWELL

References for Further Exploration

VIRTUAL MUSEUMS

Metropolitan Museum of Art (New York, NY)
http://www.metmuseum.org/

Museum of Modern Art (New York, NY)
http://www.moma.org/

Whitney Museum of American Art (New York, NY)
http://www.whitney.org/

Brooklyn Museum (Brooklyn, NY)
http://www.brooklynmuseum.org/

Carnegie Museum of Art (Pittsburgh, PA)
http://www.cmoa.org/

Philadelphia Museum of Art (Philadelphia, PA)
http://www.philamuseum.org/

Museum of Fine Arts (Boston, MA) http://www.mfa.org/

Museum of Fine Arts (Houston, TX) http://www.mfah.org

Seattle Art Museum (Seattle, WA)
http://www.seattleartmuseum.org/

Fine Arts Museums of San Francisco (San Francisco, CA)
http://www.thinker.org

San Diego Museum of Art (San Diego, CA)
http://www.sdmart.org/

Cleveland Museum of Art (Cleveland, OH)
http://www.clemusart.com/

PROFESSIONAL ORGANIZATIONS

Studio Art Quilt Associates http://www.saqa.com/

Quilt Surface Design International http://www.qsds.com

International Quilt Association http://www.quilts.org/

Surface Design Association http://www.surfacedesign.org/

Professional Art Quilters Alliance
http://www.artquilters.com/

PUBLICATIONS

Crawford, Tad. *Legal Guide for the Visual Artist.* Allworth Press: New York 1999.

Michels, Caroll. *How to Survive and Prosper as an Artist: Selling Yourself Without Selling Your Soul.* Owl Books: New York 2001.

Smith, Constance. *Art Marketing 101.* North Light Books: Cincinnati 2000.

Smith, Constance, and Sue Viders. *Art Office.* ArtNetwork Press: Penn Valley 1998.

Art Calendar magazine http://www.artcalendar.com/

Crafts Report magazine http://www.craftsreport.com/

Professional Quilter magazine
http://www.professionalquilter.com/

Chapter 11 Homework

Research shows or exhibits you would like to enter and request application information. Make stuff!

STUDENT GALLERY

The art quilts in the following gallery are a sampling of the work from the student exhibitions of our class titled Art Quilting 101. This ten-week course, covering all the topics found in this book, culminates in an exhibit following each session. Students are encouraged to make up to six quilts within a theme and follow the 9″ × 12″ size requirement.

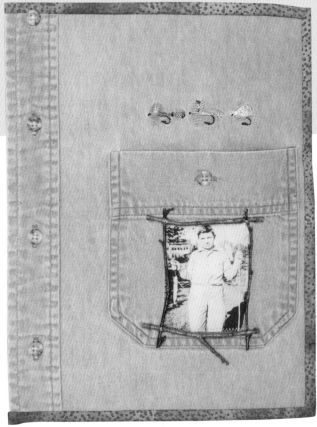

ABL, by Karen Lowry Reed

Derwent Gifts, by Karen Lowry Reed

Goodbye, by Karen Lowry Reed

Postcards From Oz: Uluru Mystique, by Susan Cox

Postcards From Oz: The Sails of Sydney, by Susan Cox

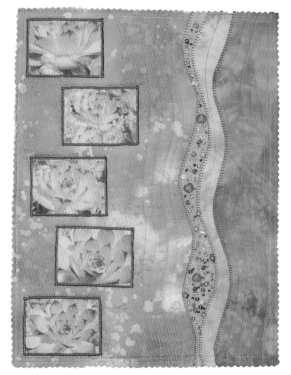

Hens & Chicks Series I, by Norma Schlager

Hens & Chicks Series II, by Norma Schlager

Traveler, by Wendy Sloneker

Reach, by Wendy Sloneker

Rest, by Wendy Sloneker

Potsie 1, by Carolyn J. Spiegel

Potsie 2, by Carolyn J. Spiegel

Nauset, by Lisa Jenner

Piping Plover, by Lisa Jenner

Tangerine Eyes, Sunset Dreams, by Cindy Silverstein

Sing the Secret of the Soul, by Cindy Silverstein

Shadows of a Lover's Dream, by Cindy Silverstein

Otoño, by Jane Dávila

acid-free—a characteristic of materials that have a pH of (or close to) 7, which makes them more permanent and less likely to discolor or deteriorate

archival—having good aging properties

brayer—a small hand roller used to spread paint or ink

burnishing tool (or burnisher)—a tool with a smooth surface, used for rubbing, smoothing, or polishing

clear acetate—transparent plastic

crop—trim

decorative/novelty thread—threads that are heavier or more dimensional than regular sewing-weight threads

hand of the fabric—the drape and softness of the fabric

mask—a covering used to conceal or protect certain portions of an image

medium—the material or technique used by an artist

negative space—the area of empty space created by the exterior lines of other elements

opaque—not transparent or translucent

organic shape—a shape associated with nature, not geometric

palette—a range of colors used by an artist; a plate used to hold pigment

piping—cording wrapped in a narrow tube of fabric used as a trim

portfolio—a case for carrying presentation materials such as drawings or photographs

presentation book—a book with clear sleeves for holding presentation materials

prospectus—a document containing rules and information about an exhibit

registration mark—a mark made to aid in the positioning, placement, or alignment of elements

scale—proportional/dimensional relationship

stretchers—wooden strips that can be joined together as a frame, over which canvas is stretched

stylize—to alter shapes, patterns, or colors to represent them in a controlled manner

textile medium—a liquid added to paint used to soften the hand of painted fabric

thumbnail sketch—a small, rough drawing

tulle—fine netting

unity—the quality of elements coming together to create a cohesive whole

viewfinder—a device used to find a focal point or area of interest

viscosity—the level of flow versus stickiness of a liquid (the thicker a liquid is, the higher its viscosity; the thinner it is, the lower its viscosity)

Blue Zuzu, by Elin Waterston

Fashionable Women, by Elin Waterston

Sometimes it's beneficial to get another artist's opinion or input on a current project. One way to do this is to join or form a critique group, where you can meet with other artists on a regular basis and discuss projects or problems or just do some brainstorming.

When working with a critique group (or even alone), the following questions can help you form constructive critiques (not criticisms) of your work and that of others. It's more helpful to ask these questions about a sketch or a work in progress, since you can still make changes easily, than about a finished piece. Ask yourself:

- Is the technique consistent? Does the piece hold together and seem unified? Is the theme, idea, or vision clear?

- What kind of balance has been used in the composition?

- Has attention been given to both positive and negative space?

- Is the background too busy? Should it be simplified?

- Have the objects in the composition been grouped in interesting ways? Are there smaller compositions within the larger compositions?

- Is there more than one focal point? If so, are the focal points fighting one another? Are there areas where the emphasis is greater than other areas?

- Is the overall composition too crowded or too empty? If so, is this intentional?

- Where should the viewer's eye travel? Have paths of movement throughout the composition been created?

- If light and value change are used in the composition, is there an identifiable direction of the light source?

RESOURCES

Flourish!—Country Quilter
344 Route 100
Somers, NY 10589
(914) 277-4820
(888) 277-7780
http://www.countryquilter.com/
Complete art-quilting supplies, fabric, fibers, books, paint, ink, stamp pads, beads, photo transfer materials

Dharma Trading
P.O. Box 150916
San Rafael, CA 94915
(800) 524-5227
http://www.dharmatrading.com/
Mail-order surface-design supplies

Blick Art Materials
P.O. Box 1267
Galesburg, IL 61402
(800) 828-4548
http://www.dickblick.com/
Mail-order art and craft supplies

Pearl Paint
(800) 451-7327
http://www.pearlpaint.com/
Mail-order art supplies

Jerry's Artarama
5325 Departure Drive
Raleigh, NC 27616
(800) 827-8478
http://www.jerrysartarama.com/
Mail-order art supplies

PRO Chemical & Dye
P.O. Box 14
Somerset, MA 02726
(800) 228-9393
http://www.prochemical.com/
Mail-order paints and dyes

Nasco Arts & Crafts
(800) 558-9595
http://www.enasco.com/artsandcrafts/
Mail-order art and craft supplies

Quilting Arts
23 Gleasondale Road
Stow, MA 01775-1319
(800) 406-5283
http://www.quiltingarts.com/
Books, magazines, surface-design supplies

Fire Mountain Gems and Beads
(800) 355-2137
http://www.firemountaingems.com/
Beads and embellishments

St. Theresa Textile Trove
5846 Hamilton Avenue
Cincinnati, OH 45224
P: (513) 333-0399
(800) 236-2450
http://www.sttheresatextile.com/
info@sttheresatextile.com
Unique fabric and embellishments

accent strip 22

acrylic gel medium 64, 67

archival considerations 64

artist's statements.................................... 83

balance 14, 39

beads.. 72

bobbin drawing 57, 61

bobbin tension 61

Bubble Jet Set 27

buttons 73

calls for entry 82

canvas stretchers 79

canvas, painted 79

charms 75

closed form 22

collage 36

   with a focus 38, 40

color... 18, 37, 49

   and cultural differences 19

   moods 19

   temperature 19, 37

   controlled palette 20

   vocabulary of 18

contracts 85

commissions 85

couching 58, 62

creative process 9

critiquing 86, 93

delivery and shipping 84

drawing.............................. 15, 16, 29, 59

from a photo 29

   fear of... 15

exhibiting 82

finishing 77

foiling 50, 53

framing your composition 22

free-motion machine embroidery 57

hand stitching 58, 66

hanging 78

inspiration 9, 25, 27, 29

   from photos 27

   from art 29

   sources of 9

insurance... 84

labels 78

marketing 84

milagros 75

negative space 15, 37, 39

networking.. 86

no-binding binding............................... 80

objects, man-made................................ 65

objects, natural....................................... 65

open form 22

organizations, professional................. 86

paint 48, 52

   acrylic... 48

   textile 48

   on colored or printed fabric........... 49

painting, freehand 49

paper... 65, 68

perspective 21, 24

photo editing... 26

photography, for exhibition 83

photography, in quilt design 25

piecing 41

   freehand curves...........................41, 43

   insert strips 42, 45

   wonky 42, 44

portfolio 83

presentation book 83

pricing... 84

printing on fabric 26

prospectus... 82

sequins.. 74, 75

shisha 73, 74

stamping 50, 52

textile medium 48

thread painting 57, 60

tools 65

tracing... 29

trims 75

using your computer 25

viewfinder 27, 28

visual elements of design..................... 13

visual principles of design 14

wire 65, 67

working in a series 12

working with a theme 11

JANE DÁVILA

Uncomfortable unless she is creating and making art, Jane began her professional art career as a printmaker, specializing in etchings and intaglios. Her prints are in many private and corporate collections. In 1990, when her mother, Claire Oehler, opened the Country Quilter and invited her to join the business, Jane began her journey into fabric and fiber.

Her artistic adventure continues, and the addition of paper to her art quilts brings her favorite media together. She teaches and designs for the Country Quilter, where watching her students discover their creativity is a great joy.

She lives in Ridgefield, Connecticut, with her husband, her daughter, and one little blonde dog.

ELIN WATERSTON

Elin taught herself to sew when she was a child and would beg her mother to take her to the fabric store. In college and graduate school, she studied costume design and worked in costume shops building costumes and masks, using all sorts of materials and painting, dyeing and manipulating fabrics. Eventually, that evolved into quilt-making, which evolved into art quilting.

Elin's quilts are in many public and private collections and have been exhibited in numerous galleries and museums. She teaches innovative and art quilting at the Country Quilter in Somers, New York, and art at the Katonah Art Center in Katonah, New York.

She lives in South Salem, New York, with her husband, her son, and two little white dogs.